AI-Powered Thesis Mastery

The Complete Graduate Guide to Transforming Your Research Journey with 25 Game-Changing Tools:

From Five-Chapter Foundation to AI-Enhanced Excellence for MS/MBA/M.Tech/M.Phil/LLM/Ph.D/D.Sc/D.Litt/LLD Students

Prof. Raghu Korrapati, Ph.D., D.Sc., D.Litt.

DIAMOND BOOKS
www.diamondbooks.in

Publisher	**:**	**Diamond Pocket Books (P) Ltd.** X-30, Okhla Industrial Area, Phase-II, New Delhi-110020
Phone	:	011-40712200
E-mail	:	wecare@diamondbooks.in
Website	:	www.diamondbooks.in
Edition	:	2025
Printed By	:	Repro (India)

AI-Powered Thesis Mastery

Author - *Dr. Raghu Korrapati*

Contact the Author:

Website: https://www.raghukorrapati.com/research

E-mail: raghu.korrapati@gmail.com

Phone: +1- (803) 422 6397 EDT **Fax:** +1-(866) 292 1949

Dedicated to

DSNLU DSP SIR

Inspiration

AI-Powered Thesis Mastery – Why This Book Matters

Over the past three decades, I've walked alongside countless bright, motivated graduate students from all corners of the world. They begin their journey with a spark of ambition, only to find themselves overwhelmed, disoriented, or even paralyzed, when faced with the challenges of developing a thesis. From topic discovery and research design to writing and publishing, the road to a successful thesis is often paved with uncertainty, isolation, and reliance on outdated methods.

This book was born out of a vision to change that.

My three decades as an educator, mentor, and lifelong learner have instilled in me a core belief: knowledge should empower, not intimidate. Now, with the rapid evolution of Artificial Intelligence (AI), we wield tools unimaginable just a few years ago. These innovations can not only accelerate academic research but also significantly enhance its depth, quality, and integrity. Yet, these tools remain underutilized in many graduate programs.

I wrote this book to bridge that gap.

The Five-Chapter Model, which I introduced in 2017, has consistently proven to be a reliable, flexible, and pedagogically sound framework for thesis writing. However, we can now elevate this model by integrating it with AI-driven discovery engines, visual citation networks, intelligent writing assistants, plagiarism detectors, and publishing advisors, thereby unlocking new possibilities. This powerful convergence of structure and innovation enables graduate students to succeed not just faster, but also with greater quality.

This book is a testament to what's possible when classical research principles meet the power of modern AI. It's for the student ready to push boundaries, for the scholar who strives for clarity, and for the institution that champions excellence.

A Personal Note to Graduate Students.

If you've ever doubted your ability to complete a thesis, let me reassure you: you absolutely can. Read my book, ***Any One Can Do A Ph.D***. With the right tools, guidance, and mindset, you won't just complete it—you'll excel.

Let's be clear: AI won't replace your intelligence; it will amplify it. This book equips you with the knowledge to use AI ethically, effectively, and purposefully, enabling you to discover ideas, rigorously test hypotheses, deeply analyze patterns, and ultimately craft a compelling research narrative that truly resonates.

Beyond a mere guidebook, this is your dedicated companion for the academic journey, crafted to support you from your current starting point and guide your evolution. It synthesizes decades of academic mentorship, practical industry experience, and a deep commitment to empowering the next generation of scholars.

Let this book be your catalyst.

- Prof. Raghu Korrapati, ***Esq., Ph.D., D.Sc., D.Litt.***

Preface

Over the last decade, Artificial Intelligence (AI) has revolutionized sectors ranging from finance to healthcare, and transportation to entertainment. Strikingly, its profound capabilities largely remain **unleashed within academia**. For graduate students, especially those embarking on a thesis or dissertation, AI presents a **transformative opportunity**—not to automate their intellectual heavy lifting, but to enable them to conduct their research with greater precision and impact.

AI-Powered Thesis Mastery is the direct result of my lifelong dedication to fostering student success. It integrates my proven **Five-Chapter Model** with over 25 meticulously selected AI tools, each designed to support every phase of the thesis journey—from identifying critical research gaps to successfully publishing your findings.

This book is your blueprint for **thesis mastery**, guiding you not merely to completion, but to true academic thriving. Designed for Master's candidates, Ph.D. scholars, and faculty mentors alike, it **demystifies the research process** and illustrates how to harness AI ethically and powerfully for **superior academic output**.

Ultimately, I hope this book drastically reduces the stress, frustration, and time commonly spent on thesis writing, ushering in an era of clarity, confidence, and productive momentum. I challenge you to **engage fully with these pages, experiment**

with the AI tools, internalize the strategies, and confidently realize your potential to produce exceptional scholarly work.

Most importantly, this book was written for those who grappling with writer's block. Writer's block is the most common challenge I've seen in students—and it's also the most beatable. The AI tools in this guide are designed to help you break through mental barriers and keep your progress flowing. In my decades of guiding research scholars, I have always shared three principles for thesis success:

1. **Don't worry about getting it right—just get it written.**
2. **Anything that is written can be improved.**
3. **Research is nothing but a read–write exercise—and anyone can do a Ph.D.**

Now, let's begin.

- Prof. Raghu Korrapati, *Esq., Ph.D., D.Sc., D.Litt.*

Table of Contents

SECTION I
Foundations of AI-Enhanced Research

PART I
AI Tools for Graduate Research Students (36 PPT Slides)

Welcome to "AI-Powered Thesis Journey," a dynamic presentation by Prof. Raghu Korrapati, Ph.D., D.Sc., D.Litt., designed to empower graduate students pursuing MS, MBA, M.Tech, M.Phil, LLM, Ph.D., D.Sc., and D.Litt. degrees. This comprehensive set of 36 slides serves as a roadmap for integrating over 25 cutting-edge AI tools into the thesis development process, aligning with the traditional five-chapter thesis model. For those unable to read the entire book, these slides offer a concise yet powerful overview, taking just 30 minutes to review and note key insights, enabling you to grasp essential AI strategies to transform your research journey.

This presentation distills the book's core concepts into an accessible, actionable format, guiding you through each research phase with targeted AI solutions. Whether you're a novice or an experienced researcher, these slides provide practical tools to enhance efficiency, elevate quality, and accelerate your path to graduation, all while maintaining academic rigor and ethical standards.

Core Benefits of AI Integration: Integrating AI tools into your thesis process offers transformative advantages:

- **Save Research Time:** Streamline tasks like literature searches, data analysis, and writing, reducing research time by up to 60%.
- **Enhance Quality:** Leverage AI-powered analysis to uncover deeper insights, improve methodological rigor, and produce polished, professional outputs.
- **Graduate Faster:** Accelerate your academic journey from research discovery to final submission, minimizing delays and boosting productivity.

These benefits are woven into each slide, ensuring you can quickly adopt AI tools to achieve measurable results.

Impact Promise: By strategically integrating these AI tools, the presentation promises to save you over 20 hours weekly, allowing more time for critical thinking and original contributions. The slides enhance research quality by enabling deeper insights, more comprehensive literature reviews, and rigorous analyses, all while accelerating your path to graduation. Even if you can't read the whole book, these 36 slides will give you the core insights in about 30 minutes, allowing you to quickly grasp key concepts and take notes.

Getting Started: To maximize the presentation's value:

1. Review the 36 slides in approximately 30 minutes, taking notes on tools relevant to your research stage.
2. Identify 2–3 high-impact tools (e.g., Semantic Scholar for literature, Grammarly for writing) to implement immediately.
3. Refer to the book's corresponding sections for deeper guidance on specific tools or stages.
4. Document your AI usage to ensure ethical compliance.

This presentation equips you with the knowledge and tools to embark on an AI-powered thesis journey, transforming your research process into a more efficient, insightful, and impactful endeavor.

Your AI-Powered Thesis Journey

Navigating the 5-Chapter Model with Intelligent Tools

25+ AI Tools for Academic Success

Presented by

Prof. Raghu Korrapati, Ph.D., D.Sc., D.Litt.

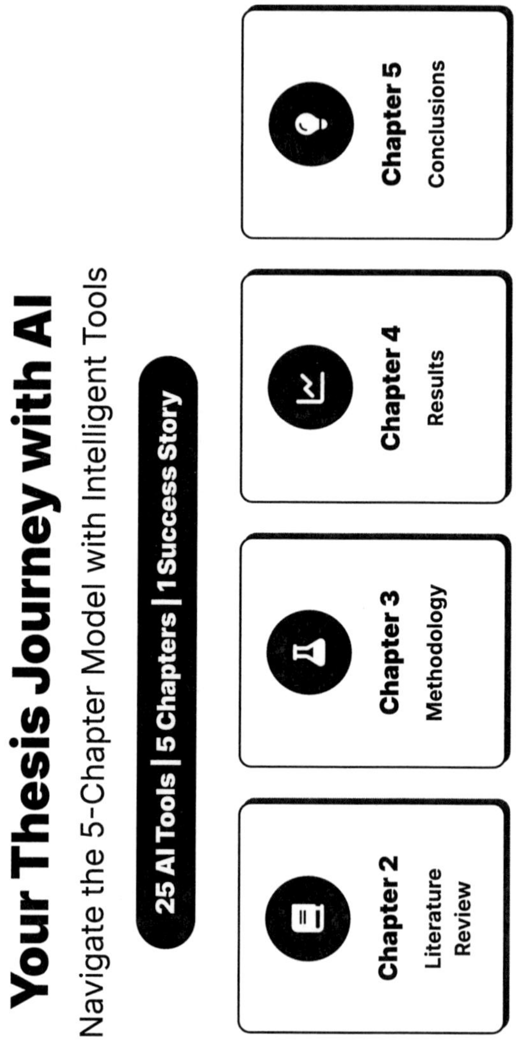
Your Thesis Journey with AI
Navigate the 5-Chapter Model with Intelligent Tools
25 AI Tools | 5 Chapters | 1 Success Story
Chapter 1
Introduction
Chapter 2
Literature Review
Chapter 3
Methodology
Chapter 4
Results
Chapter 5
Conclusions

Chapter 1

1 Research Discovery Tools

AI-powered tools to efficiently discover, explore, and navigate academic research resources

Knowledge Discovery | Research Navigation | Note Organization

---

Find relevant academic papers and resources using AI-powered search algorithms

Navigate complex research landscapes and identify connections between related works

Organize, annotate, and structure research findings for comprehensive thesis development

Semantic Scholar

AI-Powered Research Engine

semanticscholar.org

○ Free & Accessible

Key Features

AI-Powered Search
Machine learning understands research context

Citation Analysis
Track patterns and impact metrics

Smart Filters
Filter by year, author, venue, field

Paper Recommendations
AI suggests relevant papers

Coverage Highlights

- Over 200 million academic papers
- Comprehensive multi-disciplinary coverage
- Focus on open access research
- Updated citation metrics

Research Rabbit

Discovery Through Exploration

researchrabbit.ai

○ Free with Registration

★ Key Features

Visual Networks

Interactive paper connection graphs

Smart Recommendations

AI-powered paper suggestions

Collections

Organize papers into themed groups

Research Alerts

Stay updated on new papers

Applications for Research

- Find unexplored research connections
- Trace evolution of research ideas
- Discover key researchers & author networks
- Perfect for comprehensive literature mapping

Undermind

AI-Powered Research Assistant

undermind.ai

○ Freemium Model

Key Features

Deep Search
Goes beyond keyword matching

AI Understanding
Comprehends research context

Smart Filtering
Relevance-based results

Multi-Source
Searches across databases

Research Applications

- Identify unexplored research gaps
- Validates research novelty
- Find comprehensive background
- Save 70% of typical research time

Napkin AI

Visual Thinking Tool

napkin.ai

Free During Beta

Key Features

Visual Mind Maps
AI-generated concept diagrams

Idea Generation
Creative brainstorming assistance

Concept Mapping
Visualize relationships & connections

Collaborative Canvas
Team ideation & visual planning

Research Applications

- Problem mapping: Visualize research problems
- Research design: Plan methodology visually
- Concept development: Build frameworks
- Creative insights: Discover new connections

Avidnote

Research Note-Taking Tool

avidnote.com

Freemium Model

Key Features

Smart Note-Taking

Academic-focused organization

Framework Builder

Theoretical structure creation

Citation Integration

Link notes to academic sources

Smart Tagging

Auto-organize research concepts

Applications for Research

- Organize research questions & concepts
- Build theoretical frameworks visually
- Link theories to research questions
- Structure literature review notes

Chapter 2

2 Literature Review Tools

AI-powered tools to systematically analyze, synthesize, and organize existing research

Literature Discovery | **Evidence Synthesis** | **Accelerated Writing**

Find comprehensive, relevant literature efficiently across multiple databases and sources

Analyze patterns, extract insights, and build coherent theoretical frameworks

Transform research insights into well-structured, academically rigorous literature reviews

Connected Papers

Visual Research Mapping

connectedpapers.com

Free Access Available

Key Features

Citation Networks
Visual maps of paper connections

Prior Works
Trace research origins

Derivative Works
Find follow-up research

Similar Papers
Discover related themes

Applications for Literature Review

- Visualize research landscape and connections
- Track evolution of ideas through citation networks
- Identify research gaps in the literature
- Discover new research directions and opportunities

R Discovery

Research Navigation & Discovery

discovery.researcher.life

○ Free & Premium Plans

Key Features

Research Pathways
Navigate literature connections

Topic Mapping
Visualize research domains

Smart Filtering
Relevance-based organization

Literature Synthesis
Combine multiple sources

Thesis Applications

Research Benefits

Research Landscape
Map knowledge domains

Theme Connections
Identify theoretical links

Research Trends
Track field evolution

Knowledge Gaps
Find research opportunities

Perfect For

- Systematic literature organization
- Theoretical framework building
- Knowledge gap identification
- Research theme visualization

Consensus AI

Evidence Synthesis & Research Consensus

consensus.app

Free & Premium Plans

Key Features

Evidence Extraction
Extract key findings from papers

Consensus Finding
Identify scientific agreement

Claim Verification
Validate research claims

Thesis Applications

Scientific Consensus
Find areas of agreement

Evidence Synthesis
Combine research findings

Knowledge Gaps
Identify research conflicts

Study Analysis
Analyze quality & bias

Perfect For

- Building theoretical frameworks
- Supporting research arguments
- Identifying research controversies

PaperPal

AI Academic Writing Assistant

paperpal.com

Free & Premium ($25/month)

Key Features

Grammar & Style
Academic writing enhancement

Language Polish
Improve clarity & readability

Citation Format
APA, MLA, Chicago styles

Thesis Applications

Academic Tone
Maintain scholarly style

Error Detection
Find grammar issues

Writing Improvement
Enhance clarity & flow

Citations
Format references properly

Perfect For

- Polishing chapter drafts
- Maintaining academic tone
- Ensuring proper citations

EnagoRead

Smart Reading Assistant

read.enago.com

Free Trial & Premium

Key Features

PDF Reading

Smart PDF analysis & navigation

Auto Summarization

Key points extraction

Translation

Multi-language support

Thesis Applications

Fast Reading

Process papers efficiently

Key Insights

Extract main findings

Organize Notes

Structure your reading

Multi-language

Overcome language barriers

Perfect For

- Reading large volumes of papers
- Understanding complex academic texts
- Organizing literature notes

Manus AI

Intelligent Research Assistant

manus.ai

Free Trial & Premium

Key Features

Smart Literature Search
AI-powered research discovery

Research Graph
Visual paper relationships

AI Insight Generation
Automated research analysis

Thesis Applications

Gap Analysis
Identify research opportunities

Literature Mapping
Visualize research landscape

Insight Generation
Automated theme detection

Literature Export
Integration with references

Perfect For

- Comprehensive literature reviews
- Finding research gaps
- Synthesizing multiple sources

Gemini Advanced AI

Google's Research Intelligence Platform

gemini.google.com

○ Free & Subscription Plans

Key Features

Multimodal Research

Text, image & data processing

Literature Analysis

Deep content understanding

Knowledge Synthesis

Connect ideas across sources

Literature Review Applications

Synthesis Mapping

Connect diverse literature

Gap Identification

Find unexplored areas

Theme Extraction

Identify research patterns

Framework Building

Theoretical foundations

Perfect For

- Complex literature analyses
- Multi-disciplinary research
- Theoretical framework building
- Research gap identification

ThesisAI

AI-Powered Academic Document Drafting

thesisai.io

Free Trial & Premium

Key Features

AI Literature Generation

Create full reviews from prompts

Bulk Paper Processing

Handle up to 100 papers at once

Automated Citations

Generate inline citations automatically

Thesis Applications

Literature Synthesis

Combine findings from sources

Research Mapping

Visualize literature connections

Theme Extraction

Identify key research themes

Research Gap Analysis

Identify unexplored areas

Perfect For

- Comprehensive literature reviews
- Systematic research synthesis
- Citation-heavy documentation

3

Chapter 3

Methodology & Analysis Tools

Design, Execute, and Analyze Your Research

Research Design | **Data Analysis** | **Content Processing**

Plan your methodology with AI-powered tools for statistical analysis and research design

Process and analyze quantitative and qualitative data efficiently

Transform raw research data into meaningful insights with AI assistance

Scholarcy

AI Research Summarization & Analysis

scholarcy.com

Free & Premium Plans

Key Features

Smart Summaries
Extracts key findings & methods

Structured Output
Organized section breakdown

Key Concepts
Automatic keyword extraction

Thesis Applications

Method Analysis
Extract research methods

Data Synthesis
Combine multiple studies

Framework Design
Structure your approach

Bulk Processing
Handle multiple papers

Perfect For

- Systematic literature reviews
- Methodology comparison
- Research framework building

NotebookLM

Google's AI Research Notebook

G notebooklm.google

○ Free with Google Account

Key Features

Multi-Source Upload
PDFs, docs, links, research notes

AI Chat Interface
Ask questions about your sources

Source Citations
Auto-linked references in responses

Thesis Applications

Source Organization
Centralize research materials

Cross-Reference
Find connections across sources

Method Comparison
Analyze different approaches

AI-Powered Insights
Discover patterns in sources

Perfect For

- Methodology notebook creation
- Multi-source analysis
- Research framework synthesis

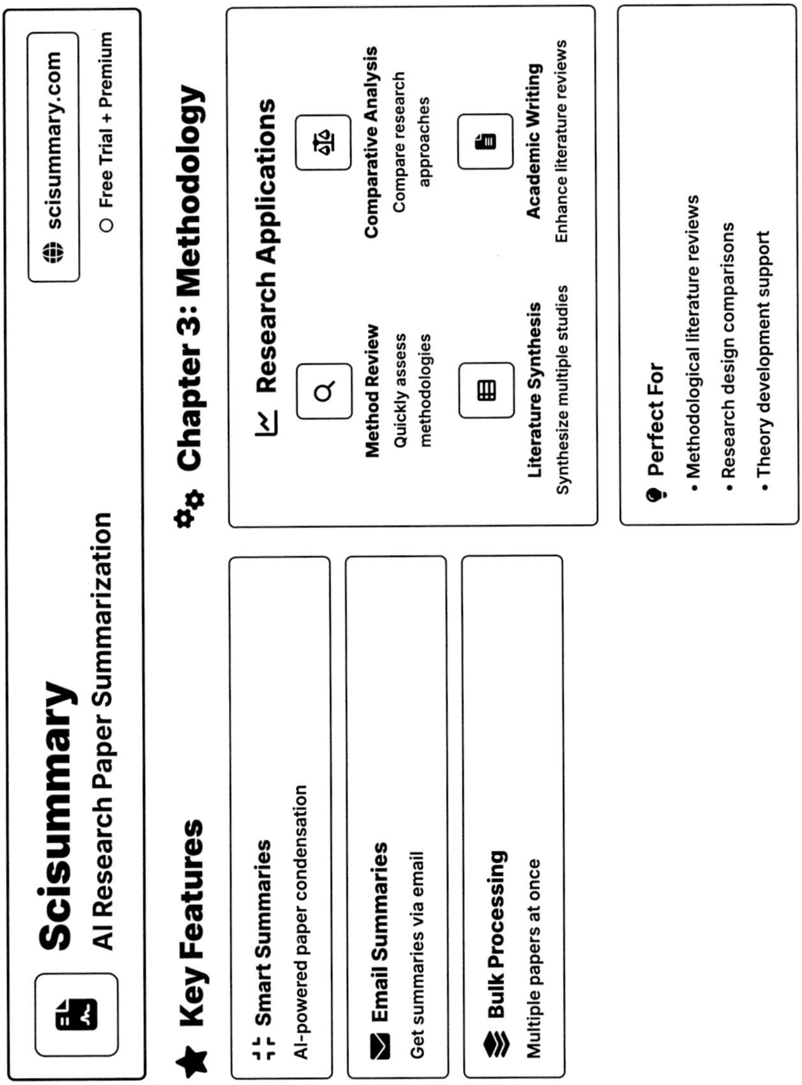
Scisummary
AI Research Paper Summarization
scisummary.com
Free Trial + Premium
Key Features
Smart Summaries
AI-powered paper condensation
Email Summaries
Get summaries via email
Bulk Processing
Multiple papers at once
Chapter 3: Methodology
Research Applications
Method Review
Quickly assess methodologies
Comparative Analysis
Compare research approaches
Literature Synthesis
Synthesize multiple studies
Academic Writing
Enhance literature reviews
Perfect For
• Methodological literature reviews
• Research design comparisons
• Theory development support

Chapter 4

4 Writing & Results Tools

Transform your drafts into polished academic writing with AI-powered writing assistants, reference managers, and result visualization tools

Academic Writing | Results Presentation | Citation Management

Craft clear, concise, and academically rigorous manuscripts that effectively communicate your research

Present your findings with impactful visualizations and properly formatted results sections

Manage references and citations seamlessly throughout your writing process

SciSpace

AI Research Assistant & Writing Tool

scispace.com

Free + Premium Plans

Key Features

Chat with Papers

Ask questions about research papers

AI Writing Assistant

Academic writing support

Citation Generator

Auto-format references

Chapter 4: Writing & Results

Thesis Applications

Draft Writing

AI-assisted content creation

Results Discussion

Interpret research findings

Reference Management

Organize citations

Complex Concepts

Explain difficult text

Perfect For

- Results chapter writing
- Discussion sections
- Citation formatting
- Understanding complex academic text

Julius AI

Data Analysis & Visualization

julius.ai

Free + Premium Plans

Key Features

File Upload
CSV, Excel, JSON support

Auto Visualization
Smart chart generation

Statistical Analysis
Descriptive & inferential stats

Chapter 4: Results

Thesis Applications

Data Visualization
Create publication-ready charts

Statistical Testing
Run hypothesis tests

Data Summary
Generate descriptive statistics

No Coding Required
Point-and-click analysis

Perfect For

- Survey data analysis
- Experimental results
- Chart creation for publications

Claude

Anthropic's AI Research Assistant

claude.ai

Free + $20/month Premium

Key Features

200K+ Token Context
Process entire research papers

Academic Writing
Scholarly tone & precise language

Content Restructuring
Reorganize & improve flow

Chapter 4: Writing & Results

Thesis Applications

Draft Generation
Create initial chapter drafts

Results Analysis
Interpret findings & trends

Literature Integration
Connect findings to research

Discussion Development
Link results to hypotheses

Perfect For

- Explaining complex research findings
- Drafting methodology & results sections
- Creating scholarly-quality content

Jenni AI

Academic Writing Assistant

jenni.ai

$20/month - Free Trial Available

Key Features

AI Writing Assistant
Smart content generation & suggestions

Research Integration
Find & cite sources automatically

Citation Support
Auto-format academic references

Chapter 4: Writing & Results

Thesis Applications

Draft Creation
AI-assisted chapter writing

Content Flow
Improve argument structure

Language Polish
Enhance clarity & precision

Academic Standards
Maintains scholarly quality

Perfect For

- Research paper writing
- Literature reviews
- Chapter drafting
- Academic editing

5 Chapter 5

Final Polish & Editing Tools

Perfecting Your Thesis Before Submission

Reference Management | Grammar & Proofreading | Formatting Tools

---

Finalize citations and references using specialized reference management tools

Ensure grammatical accuracy and language clarity with AI-powered proofreading

Format your thesis according to institutional requirements and academic standards

Grammarly

AI-Powered Writing Assistant

grammarly.com

Free + Premium ($12/mo annual)

Key Features

Grammar Check

Advanced error detection & correction

Style Suggestions

Improve clarity & engagement

Tone Detection

Ensure appropriate academic tone

Plagiarism Check

Original content verification

Chapter 5: Final Polish

Thesis Applications

Final Proofreading

Error-free final draft

Style Refinement

Polish academic language

Quality Assurance

Professional presentation

Submission Ready

Publication quality

Perfect For

- Final thesis review
- Chapter polishing
- Academic writing
- Error elimination

Writefull

AI Academic Writing Assistant

writefull.com

Free + Premium Plans

Key Features

Academic Language

Field-specific scholarly phrasing

Paraphrasing Tool

Transform text into academic style

Grammar Feedback

Specialized for research writing

Abstract Generator

Create research paper abstracts

Chapter 5: Final Polish

Thesis Applications

Academic Refinement

Scholarly language enhancement

Clarity Check

Ensure research clarity

Field-Specific

Discipline-appropriate terminology

ESL Support

Ideal for non-native writers

Perfect For

- Final thesis polish
- Academic transformation
- Language consistency
- Publication preparation

Turnitin

Academic Integrity & Plagiarism Detection

turnitin.com

○ Institutional Licenses

Key Features

Originality Check
Comprehensive plagiarism detection

Vast Database
Checks against billions of sources

Similarity Score
Clear originality metrics

Detailed Reports
Source identification & highlighting

Chapter 5: Final Polish

Thesis Applications

Academic Integrity
Verify original research

Citation Check
Ensure proper attribution

Submission Security
Meet institutional standards

Quality Assurance
Credibility validation

Perfect For

- Final thesis verification
- Originality confirmation
- Pre-submission checks
- Institutional compliance

Miscellaneous Tools

Additional Research & Writing Tools

Bonus Tools

Note-Taking & Knowledge

Obsidian

obsidian.md

Connected note-taking with graph view

Notion

notion.so

All-in-one workspace

Reference Management

Mendeley

mendeley.com

Reference manager with social features

EndNote

endnote.com

Academic citation standard

Writing & Typesetting

Scrivener

literatureandlatte.com

Long-form writing organization

Overleaf

overleaf.com

Online LaTeX editor

Data & Analysis

ATLAS.ti

atlasti.com

Qualitative data analysis

NVivo

qsrinternational.com

Qualitative research analysis

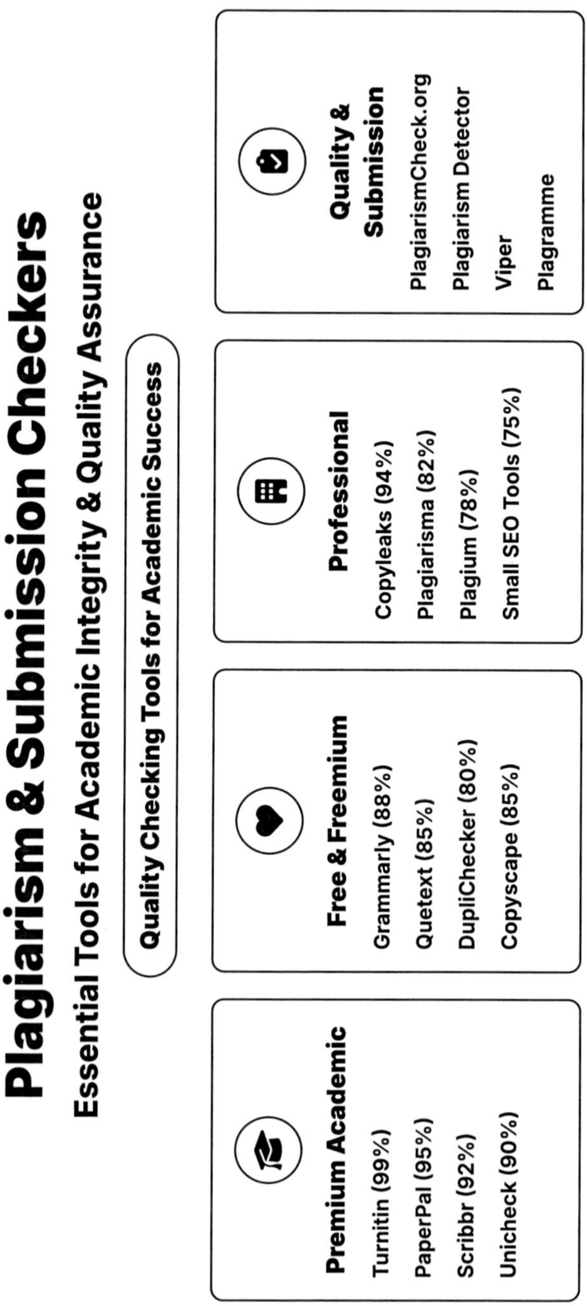
Plagiarism & Submission Checkers
Essential Tools for Academic Integrity & Quality Assurance
Quality Checking Tools for Academic Success
Premium Academic
Turnitin (99%)
PaperPal (95%)
Scribbr (92%)
Unicheck (90%)
Free & Freemium
Grammarly (88%)
Quetext (85%)
DupliChecker (80%)
Copyscape (85%)
Professional
Copyleaks (94%)
Plagiarisma (82%)
Plagium (78%)
Small SEO Tools (75%)
Quality & Submission
PlagiarismCheck.org
Plagiarism Detector
Viper
Plagramme

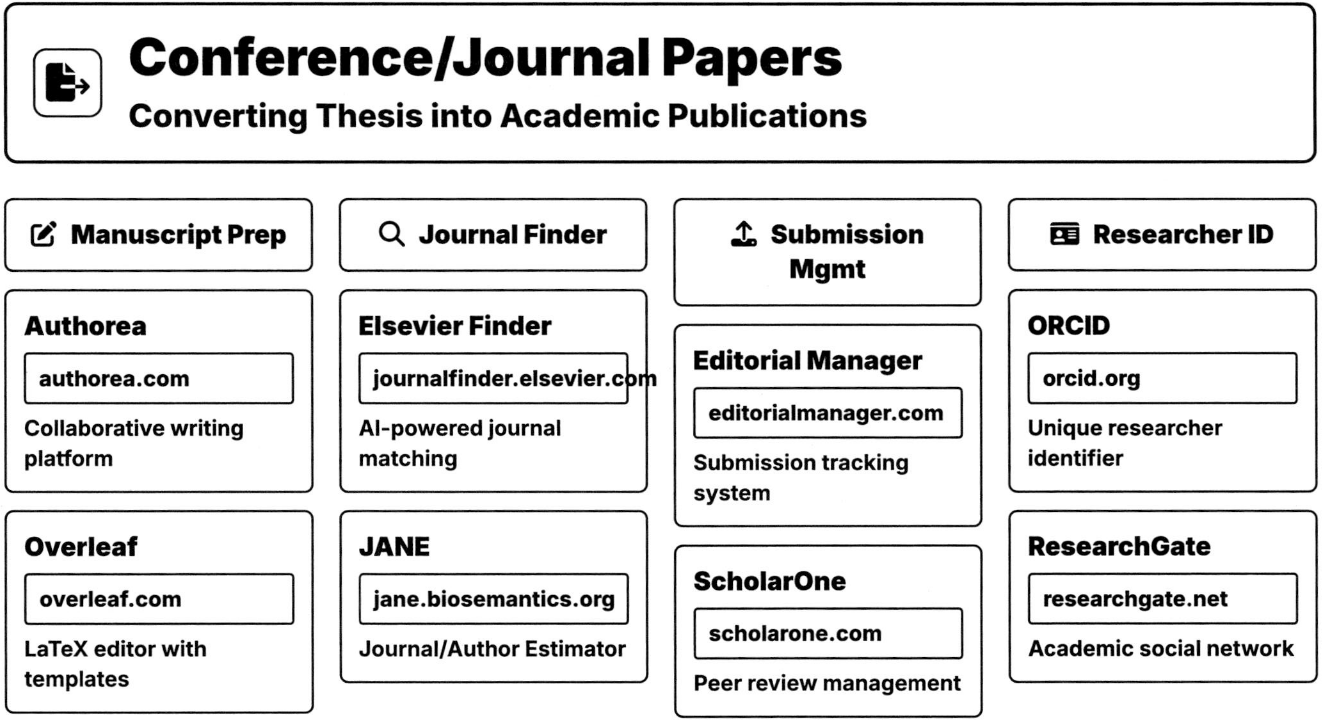
Conference/Journal Papers
Converting Thesis into Academic Publications
Manuscript Prep
Authorea
authorea.com
Collaborative writing platform
Overleaf
overleaf.com
LaTeX editor with templates
Journal Finder
Elsevier Finder
journalfinder.elsevier.com
AI-powered journal matching
JANE
jane.biosemantics.org
Journal/Author Estimator
Submission Mgmt
Editorial Manager
editorialmanager.com
Submission tracking system
ScholarOne
scholarone.com
Peer review management
Researcher ID
ORCID
orcid.org
Unique researcher identifier
ResearchGate
researchgate.net
Academic social network

Publication Opportunities

Essential Web Portals for Finding Conferences & Journals Across All Disciplines

Global Research Dissemination Resources

Major Directories

Cabell's Directory
cabells.com
Journal profiles, predatory alerts

Directory of Open Access
doaj.org
15,000+ open access journals

Humanities

H-Net Academic
h-net.org
Humanities conference listings

MLA Bibliography
mla.org
Literature & cultural studies

Engineering & CS

IEEE Xplore Events
ieee.org/conferences
Engineering conferences

ACM Digital Library
dl.acm.org
Computer science conferences

Law & Business

SSRN
ssrn.com
Legal & business preprints

Academy of Management
aom.org
Management research

Publishing Nuances - Academic Keywords Decoded

Essential Publishing Terminology Every Graduate Student Must Know

Decoding Academic Publishing Success

Indexing & Databases

Scopus

Elsevier's citation database covering 25,000+ journals

- **Gold standard for research evaluation**

Web of Science

Clarivate's premium database with strict quality criteria

- **Prestigious indexing standard**

Journal Metrics

Impact Factor (IF)

Average citations per article over 2 years

- **Good: IF > 3.0**
- **Excellent: IF > 10.0**

CiteScore

Scopus alternative to IF with 4-year citation window

- **More inclusive than Impact Factor**

Author Metrics

H-Index

H papers with at least H citations each

- **PhD Graduate: H = 5-10**
- **Full Professor: H = 20-50+**

ORCID ID

Unique researcher identifier linking all publications

- **Required by most journals**

Citation Impact

Citation Count

Total times a paper has been cited

- **Good paper: 10+ citations**
- **High impact: 50+ citations**

Open Access Impact

OA papers typically receive 18% more citations

- **Significant citation advantage**

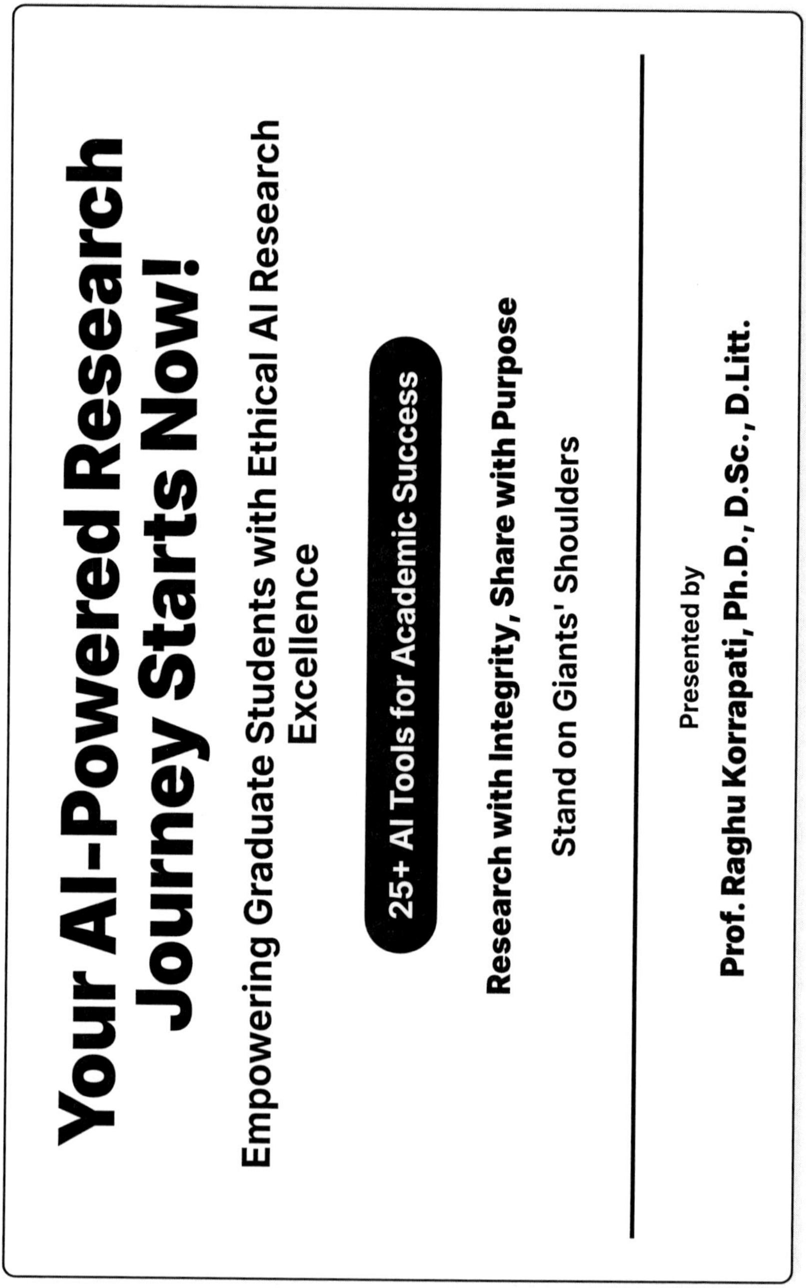
Your AI-Powered Research Journey Starts Now!
Empowering Graduate Students with Ethical AI Research Excellence
25+ AI Tools for Academic Success
Research with Integrity, Share with Purpose
Stand on Giants' Shoulders
Presented by
Prof. Raghu Korrapati, Ph.D., D.Sc., D.Litt.

PART II
The AI Revolution in Academic Research

A. Introduction to AI in Scholarly Inquiry

The integration of artificial intelligence (AI) into academic research marks a transformative shift in scholarly inquiry, rivaling the impact of digital databases. This revolution transcends mere tool adoption, fundamentally redefining how graduate students across MS, MBA, M.Tech, M.Phil, LLM, Ph.D., D.Sc., and D.Litt. programs discover, analyze, synthesize, and communicate knowledge. By automating repetitive tasks and enhancing cognitive capabilities, AI empowers researchers to produce more efficient, comprehensive, and insightful scholarship.

Traditional research processes, while rigorous, create inefficiencies that limit productivity. Graduate students typically dedicate 60–70% of their time to routine tasks—literature searches, paper summarization, citation management, and formatting—reducing scope for critical thinking or original analysis. The exponential growth of academic publications, doubling approximately every 12 years with over 3 million new papers published annually as of 2025, overwhelms manual review methods. Additionally, the increasing demand for interdisciplinary research requires synthesis across diverse fields, a challenge traditional approaches struggle to address due to varying terminologies, methodologies, and publication patterns.

AI-enhanced research mitigates these bottlenecks by streamlining workflows and amplifying human intellect. Key advantages include:

AI-enhanced Research Advantages

- **Comprehensive Literature Discovery:** AI tools process millions of papers in seconds, uncovering relevant studies and cross-disciplinary connections that traditional keyword searches often miss (e.g., Semantic Scholar, Research Rabbit).
- **Intelligent Synthesis and Gap Identification:** Advanced algorithms detect patterns, contradictions, and research gaps across vast datasets, condensing months of manual analysis into hours.
- **Accelerated Data Analysis:** AI-driven platforms (e.g., Tableau, IBM SPSS with AI) perform complex statistical operations and generate publication-ready visualizations rapidly.
- **Enhanced Writing and Editing:** AI writing assistants (e.g., Grammarly, ProWritingAid) refine academic tone, ensure clarity, and preserve the researcher's unique voice while improving grammatical accuracy.

Systematic Organization: AI-powered tools like Zotero or Obsidian create dynamic, searchable repositories for references and notes, enhancing research efficiency over time.

These capabilities enable researchers to focus on high-value tasks: formulating research questions, developing theoretical frameworks, and generating original insights.

The adoption of AI in research raises valid concerns about academic integrity, originality, and skill development, which must be addressed through responsible implementation. When used transparently, AI tools strengthen scholarship by enabling thorough literature reviews, accurate citations, and robust analysis. Clear documentation of AI use ensures integrity. By automating routine tasks, AI frees researchers to engage in creative problem-solving and theoretical innovation, with the researcher remaining the source of interpretive and conceptual contributions. AI tools also serve as learning accelerators, providing real-time feedback, suggesting advanced techniques, and exposing researchers to sophisticated analytical methods that enhance expertise. However, researchers must critically evaluate AI outputs for biases or inaccuracies, ensuring human judgment guides final decisions.

The most effective approach to AI-enhanced research is a partnership model, where researchers retain control over research design, theoretical frameworks, and interpretive analysis while leveraging AI for efficiency. AI serves as a powerful assistant—handling data processing, pattern recognition, and task automation—while the researcher's expertise, creativity, and critical thinking remain central to the process.

As AI technology evolves, its role in academia will expand, offering enhanced predictive modeling, real-time global collaboration, and personalized research workflows. However, researchers must balance AI adoption with ethical considerations to ensure tools amplify, rather than replace, human scholarship. This partnership empowers graduate students to navigate the complexities of modern research, producing high-quality work that contributes meaningfully to their fields.

B. Understanding the Five-Chapter Thesis Model

The five-chapter thesis model is a cornerstone of doctoral dissertations and master's theses across disciplines, providing a structured, logical progression from problem identification to conclusions. This time-tested framework ensures a coherent narrative that guides readers through the research process. Understanding its components is critical for leveraging AI tools effectively, as each chapter offers distinct opportunities for technological enhancement while maintaining academic rigor.

The Five-Chapter Model

Chapter 1: Introduction- Defines the research problem and its significance, articulates research objectives and questions, outlines the study's scope, limitations, and organization.

Chapter 2: Literature Review- Synthesizes relevant existing research, identifies theoretical frameworks and methodological approaches, establishes the research gap, and formulates hypotheses or research propositions.

Chapter 3: Methodology- Justifies the research design and approach, details data collection methods, instruments, and procedures, describes analytical techniques, and addresses validity, reliability, and ethical considerations.

Chapter 4: Results- Presents findings from data analysis objectively, includes tables, figures, and statistical outputs aligned with research questions, and avoids interpretation to maintain focus on raw findings.

Chapter 5: Summary, Conclusions, and Further Research- Interprets results in the context of existing literature, discusses implications for theory, practice, and policy, acknowledges limitations, proposes future research directions, and summarizes the study's contributions.

AI tools align seamlessly with this structure, enhancing efficiency and depth while preserving scholarly standards. For the Introduction, AI-powered research discovery tools (e.g., Semantic Scholar, Research Rabbit) streamline problem identification by analyzing vast datasets to highlight gaps and trends, while visualization tools like Napkin or Miro assist in organizing concepts for clearer objective articulation. In the Literature Review, AI-driven platforms revolutionize evidence synthesis by processing thousands of papers simultaneously, identifying patterns, contradictions, and gaps, and generating concise summaries to inform theoretical frameworks.

For Methodology, tools analyze methodological trends, suggest rigorous approaches, and assist in designing protocols and ensuring ethical compliance. In the Results chapter, AI-powered platforms automate complex statistical analyses and produce publication-ready visualizations, with natural language processing translating data patterns into clear narratives. For the Summary, Conclusions, and Further Research, AI writing tools enhance discussion development, ensuring logical flow and academic tone, while reference management systems ensure citation accuracy and predictive tools suggest future research directions.

Integrating AI within the five-chapter model upholds traditional academic standards while enhancing efficiency. AI tools support, rather than replace, scholarly rigor by automating repetitive tasks and providing deeper insights. Researchers remain responsible for theoretical development, methodological decisions, analytical interpretation, and scholarly synthesis, ensuring theses meet institutional expectations. The five-chapter model provides a structured backbone, but AI introduces flexibility to explore comprehensive literature reviews, test alternative methodologies, conduct advanced analyses, and craft nuanced discussions. This approach allows researchers to produce technologically sophisticated work that adheres to traditional expectations, satisfying thesis committees while showcasing enhanced scholarship.

By leveraging AI, researchers can accelerate time-intensive tasks, enhance the depth and breadth of literature reviews and analyses, produce polished outputs with minimal effort, and address complex, interdisciplinary research questions with confidence. This synergy results in theses that are both academically robust and innovative, positioning graduate students to make meaningful contributions to their fields.

C. Benefits of AI Integration in Research

The integration of AI tools into graduate research delivers transformative benefits, enhancing efficiency, quality, and impact while fostering skill development and career growth. These advantages empower researchers across MS, MBA, M.Tech, M.Phil, LLM, Ph.D., D.Sc., and D.Litt. programs to produce superior scholarship and build lasting research capabilities.

AI tools significantly reduce the time spent on routine tasks. Literature review platforms cut review time by 60–70% by processing thousands of papers to identify relevant studies and gaps, surpassing traditional search methods. Data analysis tools perform complex statistical operations and visualizations in minutes, compared to hours of manual work, freeing time for deeper interpretation. AI writing assistants reduce editing time by 40–50%, ensuring grammatical precision and consistent academic tone. Automated citation tools eliminate 80% of manual formatting tasks, ensuring accuracy across citation styles. AI-powered note-taking systems create searchable knowledge bases, reducing information retrieval time by 50–60%.

Beyond efficiency, AI enhances research quality. By analyzing vast datasets, AI tools ensure comprehensive literature coverage, revealing patterns and connections that inform robust theoretical frameworks. AI-assisted methodology tools (e.g., Scholarcy) recommend rigorous approaches, validate designs, and align with field-specific best practices. Advanced analytics enable exploration of complex data relationships, yielding nuanced insights even for researchers with limited technical expertise. AI's ability to identify cross-disciplinary insights supports innovative, interdisciplinary frameworks. Additionally, automated tools minimize errors in citations, calculations, and organization, producing polished, professional outputs.

AI tools also accelerate skill development. Exposure to advanced statistical and analytical techniques via AI platforms expands researchers' methodological expertise. Real-time feedback from writing assistants hones academic writing skills, while literature analysis tools sharpen pattern recognition and gap identification. By embedding best practices, AI helps researchers avoid common pitfalls, fostering adoption of proven strategies.

The impact of AI-enhanced research extends to dissemination and career development. AI-assisted theses require fewer revisions due to high-quality writing, analysis, and formatting, streamlining publication. Tools like Connected Papers optimize journal selection and keyword strategies, enhancing discoverability. Collaborative platforms with AI features support teamwork and version control, fostering effective partnerships. Proficiency in AI tools demonstrates technological competence, a transferable skill valued in academic and professional settings. Researchers who master AI integration gain a competitive edge, producing high-quality work efficiently and adapting to innovative environments.

Finally, AI creates lasting knowledge assets. Searchable, AI-organized research repositories serve as personal libraries for future projects. Theoretical and methodological frameworks developed with AI can be reused, while AI-driven networking tools connect researchers with collaborators, building professional networks. These cumulative benefits empower graduate students to produce exceptional theses and develop enduring research capabilities that enhance their academic and professional journeys.

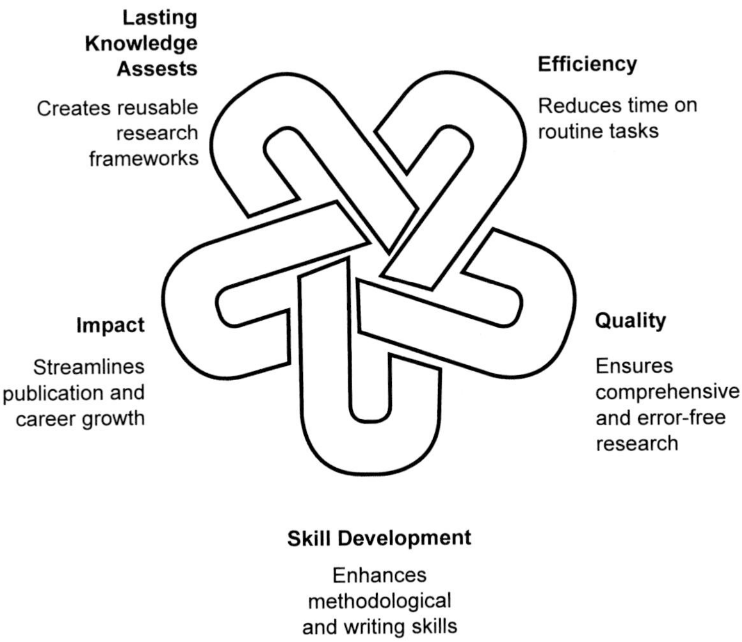

Benefits of AI Integration in Research

D. Ethical Considerations and Best Practices

The integration of artificial intelligence (AI) tools into graduate research offers transformative potential for students pursuing MS, MBA, M.Tech, M.Phil, LLM, Ph.D., D.Sc., and

D.Litt. degrees. However, to harness these tools responsibly, researchers must anchor their use in a robust ethical framework that upholds the integrity of scholarly inquiry. This section provides a comprehensive exploration of the ethical principles, best practices, and practical guidelines necessary to ensure AI enhances research while preserving academic standards, fostering transparency, and maintaining the researcher's intellectual authority.

Fundamental Ethical Principles: Ethical AI use in academic research hinges on several core principles that safeguard the credibility and authenticity of scholarly work. Transparency and attribution are paramount. Researchers must clearly document the use of AI tools, specifying the platforms employed (e.g., Semantic Scholar, Grammarly), their functionalities, and their contributions to the research process, such as literature analysis or text refinement. This transparency enables advisors, reviewers, and readers to assess the methodology and ensure the research adheres to academic standards. For example, noting that an AI tool like Research Rabbit was used to identify literature gaps provides clarity without diminishing the researcher's role in interpreting those findings.

Human agency and control form the cornerstone of ethical AI integration. AI tools should augment, not supplant, human judgment. Researchers must retain full responsibility for critical decisions, including the formulation of research questions, selection of theoretical frameworks, methodological design, and interpretation of results. AI can streamline data processing or suggest analytical approaches, but the researcher's expertise drives the intellectual direction of the study. This ensures that AI remains a supportive tool rather than a decision-maker, preserving the human element central to scholarly inquiry.

Academic integrity is non-negotiable. AI use must comply with institutional policies, disciplinary norms, and publication guidelines. This includes citing AI assistance appropriately, ensuring the final work reflects the researcher's intellectual contribution, and avoiding any misrepresentation of AI-generated content as original work. Institutions often have specific guidelines on AI use, and researchers must familiarize themselves with these to avoid unintentional violations. For instance, using AI to summarize literature is acceptable if disclosed, but presenting AI-generated text as one's own constitutes plagiarism.

Quality and accuracy remain the researcher's responsibility. AI tools, while powerful, are not infallible; they may produce errors, biases, or outdated information. Researchers must rigorously verify AI-generated outputs, such as statistical analyses or literature summaries, against primary sources to ensure validity and reliability. This diligence ensures that AI-enhanced research meets the high standards expected in graduate-level scholarship.

Best Practices for Ethical AI Use: To operationalize these principles, researchers should adopt the following best practices:

- **Documentation and Record-Keeping:** Comprehensive documentation is essential for transparency. Researchers should maintain detailed records of AI tool usage, including the specific platforms (e.g., Elicit for literature synthesis, Zotero for reference management), features utilized, and their contributions to the research. For example, if an AI tool generates a summary of 50 papers, researchers should document how that summary was modified or integrated into the literature review. Version histories should be preserved to track the evolution of

AI-assisted work, and original sources must be cited alongside AI contributions to maintain traceability.

- **Verification and Validation:** AI outputs require thorough scrutiny. Summaries generated by tools like Scholarcy should be cross-checked against original texts to confirm accuracy and relevance. Statistical analyses from platforms like Julius AI must be independently verified to ensure correctness, especially for complex datasets. AI-suggested citations and references should be validated against primary sources, and AI-assisted writing must be reviewed for tone, accuracy, and alignment with the researcher's intent. This multi-step validation process mitigates risks of errors or biases in AI outputs.
- **Appropriate Attribution:** Acknowledging AI contributions is critical to ethical research. Researchers should include AI tool usage in methodology sections, following institutional and publication guidelines. For instance, a thesis might note that Connected Papers was used to map literature connections, while Grammarly refined the text's clarity. Distinguishing between AI-assisted (e.g., grammar corrections) and AI-generated (e.g., drafted text) content is essential, as is providing specific details about the extent of AI involvement to avoid ambiguity.
- **Institutional Compliance:** Researchers must align AI use with institutional policies, which may vary across universities and disciplines. Consulting advisors and committee members early in the research process helps clarify acceptable practices, especially for sensitive areas like human subject research, where AI tools may require ethics board approval. Disciplinary standards, such as those in STEM or humanities, should also guide AI integration to ensure alignment with field-specific expectations.

Common Ethical Pitfalls to Avoid: Several pitfalls can undermine ethical AI use, and researchers must be proactive in avoiding them. Over-reliance on AI risks diminishing critical thinking and intellectual development. For example, relying solely on AI to generate research questions or analyses without human oversight can produce shallow or misaligned outcomes. AI should enhance, not replace, the researcher's analytical and creative contributions.

Inadequate verification is a significant concern. AI tools may generate plausible but inaccurate content, such as outdated references or biased summaries. Failing to verify these outputs against reliable sources can compromise research quality. For instance, an AI-generated statistical result must be checked using manual calculations or alternative software to confirm accuracy.

Unclear attribution can lead to accusations of academic dishonesty. If AI contributions are not explicitly documented, readers may assume the work is entirely the researcher's, which violates integrity standards. For example, presenting an AI-drafted paragraph without acknowledgment is unethical, even if edited.

Privacy and confidentiality violations are critical risks when using cloud-based AI tools. Uploading sensitive data, such as proprietary research or participant information, to platforms without understanding their data storage policies can breach confidentiality. Researchers should review privacy agreements and opt for tools with robust security measures, such as end-to-end encryption, when handling sensitive data.

Plagiarism through AI occurs when AI-generated content is presented as original without proper attribution. For instance, using an AI tool like Jenni to draft a literature review section and failing to disclose its role constitutes plagiarism. Researchers must clearly identify and cite AI-generated content to maintain academic honesty.

Common Ethical in AI Use

<u>Guidelines for Different Types of AI Assistance</u>: Different AI applications require tailored ethical approaches:

- **Literature Discovery and Search:** Tools like Semantic Scholar or Research Rabbit are typically considered research methods, requiring documentation in methodology sections rather than content attribution. However, any AI-generated summaries or analyses must be attributed and verified against original sources.
- **Data Analysis and Visualization:** AI-assisted statistical tools (e.g., SciSpace) require documentation of the tools used and independent verification of results. While AI may suggest analytical approaches, the interpretation and conclusions must reflect the researcher's intellectual work.
- **Writing and Editing:** AI writing assistance ranges from minor grammar corrections (minimal attribution needed) to substantial content generation (requiring clear attribution). For example, using Grammarly for proofreading requires less disclosure than using Jenni to draft entire sections, which must be explicitly noted.

- **Reference Management:** Tools like Zotero or Mendeley streamline citation processes and typically require acknowledgment in methodology sections. If AI significantly influences source selection or analysis, this contribution must be detailed.

Developing Ethical AI Practices: To ensure consistent ethical AI use, researchers should develop personal guidelines aligned with institutional and disciplinary norms. These guidelines should specify when AI tools will be used, how their contributions will be attributed, and what verification steps will be taken. For example, a researcher might decide to use AI for literature searches but manually verify all summaries before inclusion.

Regular consultation with advisors, committee members, and peers is crucial. These discussions can uncover potential ethical challenges, such as discipline-specific restrictions on AI use, and ensure alignment with academic expectations. For instance, a STEM researcher might need to address stricter data validation requirements than a humanities scholar.

Staying informed about evolving AI policies is essential in this rapidly changing field. Institutional guidelines, publication standards, and disciplinary norms are continually updated as AI adoption grows. Researchers should monitor resources like university ethics boards or journal policies to remain compliant. For example, some journals now require detailed AI usage disclosures in manuscript submissions.

In summary, Ethical AI integration enhances scholarly capabilities while upholding the core values of academic inquiry: intellectual honesty, original contribution, and rigorous methodology. By adhering to principles of transparency, human agency, academic integrity, and quality assurance, researchers can leverage AI to produce comprehensive, efficient, and impactful research. Through meticulous documentation, verification, attribution, and compliance, graduate students can navigate the ethical complexities of AI use, ensuring their work meets the highest scholarly standards while harnessing the full potential of AI tools.

E. How to Use This Guide

This comprehensive guide is crafted to serve as both a sequential learning resource and a practical reference manual for graduate students pursuing MS, MBA, M.Tech, M.Phil, LLM, Ph.D., D.Sc., and D.Litt. degrees, navigating their thesis or dissertation journey with AI-enhanced tools. Its flexible structure accommodates researchers at various stages, from beginners to advanced scholars, and supports diverse technical comfort levels and disciplinary needs. By offering clear pathways for AI tool integration, the guide empowers students to enhance efficiency, quality, and impact while maintaining academic rigor and ethical standards. Below is a detailed exploration of how to effectively utilize this guide to transform your research process.

Guide Structure and Organization: The guide is organized to support multiple approaches to learning and implementation, ensuring accessibility for all researchers. For those new to AI-enhanced research, a sequential learning path provides a structured introduction, starting with foundational concepts in Section I (AI tools and the research revolution) and progressing to practical applications in Section II (the five-chapter thesis framework) and Section III (ethical and publishing considerations). This linear approach builds a progressive understanding, ideal for students unfamiliar with AI tools or those seeking a comprehensive foundation.

Experienced researchers can adopt a targeted reference approach, focusing on specific sections or chapters relevant to their current thesis stage. Each chapter is designed to function independently while contributing to the broader framework, allowing users to dive into areas like literature review tools or data analysis platforms without needing to read the entire guide. Cross-references ensure seamless navigation between related topics.

For those eager to begin immediately, quick-start guides embedded in each major section offer condensed instructions for rapid tool adoption. These guides highlight essential tools and techniques, enabling researchers to implement AI solutions swiftly while retaining the option to explore deeper content later. This flexibility ensures the guide meets the needs of both novice and seasoned researchers.

Reading Recommendations by Research Stage: To maximize the guide's utility, tailor your reading to your current research stage:

- **Beginning Researchers (Pre-Proposal Stage):** Start with Section I to grasp the fundamentals of AI in research. Focus on research discovery tools like Semantic Scholar and Research Rabbit to identify relevant literature and gaps. Implement basic organization systems, such as Zotero for reference management or Obsidian for note-taking, to establish efficient workflows. Early attention to ethical guidelines (Section III) ensures responsible AI use from the outset, setting a strong foundation for your thesis.
- **Early-Stage Researchers (Post-Proposal, Pre-Literature Review):** Revisit Section I for context, then prioritize Section II's Chapter 2 on literature reviews. Leverage tools like Connected Papers, Consensus, or Elicit to streamline evidence synthesis and identify

theoretical frameworks. Develop systematic workflows for organizing sources and establish advanced reference management practices to maintain accuracy and efficiency.

- **Mid-Stage Researchers (Literature Review Complete, Developing Methodology):** Focus on Section II's Chapter 3 to explore methodology development tools like Scholarcy, which suggest rigorous approaches based on literature trends. Use AI to plan data collection and preliminary analyses, refining documentation and attribution practices to ensure ethical compliance. These steps prepare you for robust research design.
- **Advanced Researchers (Data Collection/Analysis Stage):** Concentrate on Section II's Chapter 4 for AI-powered data analysis tools like Julius AI or SciSpace, which automate statistical analyses and visualizations. Begin drafting results with AI assistance, ensuring objective presentation, and prepare for the transition to writing and interpretation, covered in subsequent chapters.
- **Final-Stage Researchers (Writing and Editing):** Focus on Section II's Chapter 5 and Section III for writing, editing, and publishing strategies. Section III's publishing guidance helps prepare manuscripts for submission, optimize journal selection, and enhance dissemination.

Implementation Strategies: The guide supports varied approaches to AI tool integration, allowing customization based on your needs and comfort level:

- **Gradual Adoption Approach:** Start with one or two high-impact tools addressing immediate challenges, such as Grammarly for writing or Zotero for citations. Gradually expand your toolkit as you gain confidence, minimizing the learning curve while building competence. This approach suits researchers cautious about overwhelming complexity.

- **Systematic Integration Approach:** Implement AI tools for one thesis chapter at a time, ensuring thorough mastery before progressing. For example, fully integrate literature review tools before moving to methodology platforms. This method provides comprehensive coverage while keeping complexity manageable, ideal for structured learners.
- **Tool-Specific Approach:** Focus on mastering individual tools with the greatest relevance to your research, such as Research Rabbit for literature discovery or Tableau for data visualization. Once proficient, explore integration opportunities across your workflow. This approach works well for researchers with specific tool requirements.

Special Features and Resources: The guide includes features to enhance usability and effectiveness:

- **Quick Reference Sections:** Each tool description includes concise summaries of key functionalities, enabling quick access during active research sessions without rereading entire chapters. For example, a reference section on Semantic Scholar outlines its search capabilities and integration tips.
- **Troubleshooting Guides:** Common challenges, such as inaccurate AI outputs or tool compatibility issues, are addressed with practical solutions. These guides minimize disruptions, allowing researchers to resolve problems without extensive external support.
- **Case Studies and Examples:** Real-world examples illustrate successful AI integration across disciplines like STEM, business, and humanities. These case studies provide adaptable models, showing how tools like Elicit or Julius AI have enhanced thesis outcomes.

- **Integration Checklists:** Step-by-step checklists ensure systematic tool implementation, covering setup, usage, and ethical considerations. These checklists prevent oversight of critical details, such as documenting AI contributions or verifying outputs.
- **Advanced Techniques:** For experienced users, advanced sections offer sophisticated strategies, such as combining multiple AI tools for complex analyses or optimizing workflows for interdisciplinary research, maximizing efficiency and impact.

Customization Guidelines: The guide is adaptable to diverse contexts:

- **Disciplinary Adaptations:** Disciplines have unique standards; for example, STEM research may prioritize statistical tools, while humanities focus on textual analysis. The guide provides tailored recommendations, such as using SciSpace for quantitative analysis in engineering or Elicit for qualitative synthesis in social sciences.
- **Institutional Variations:** Universities have varying AI policies. The guide offers frameworks to align tool use with institutional guidelines, ensuring compliance with ethics boards or departmental standards. Consult advisors to adapt recommendations to your institution's requirements.
- **Personal Workflow Integration:** Researchers have distinct working styles and technical proficiencies. The guide suggests customizing tool selection and integration to match preferences, such as using Notion for visual thinkers or Obsidian for text-based organizers.

Ongoing Support and Updates: The AI landscape evolves rapidly, with new tools and updates emerging frequently. The guide provides strategies for evaluating new tools, updating workflows, and staying current with best practices. Resources like online communities, tool documentation, and academic forums are recommended to keep abreast of advancements. For instance, subscribing to updates from platforms like Research Rabbit ensures access to new features.

Community and Collaboration: AI-enhanced research thrives on collaboration. The guide encourages connecting with other AI-using researchers through academic networks, conferences, or online platforms. Sharing experiences and learning from peers fosters collective expertise, enhancing tool adoption and innovation.

Success Metrics: To evaluate AI integration, the guide includes frameworks for measuring success, such as time saved, quality improvements, or publication outcomes. Regular assessment helps identify areas for refinement, ensuring optimal tool use. For example, tracking literature review efficiency with Elicit can quantify time savings and comprehensiveness gains.

Getting Started: Begin your AI-enhanced research journey by:

AI-Enhanced Research Journey

1. Assessing your research stage and primary challenges (e.g., literature overload, data analysis complexity).
2. Selecting 2–3 high-impact tools, such as Semantic Scholar for literature or Grammarly for writing.
3. Implementing these tools with proper documentation, following ethical guidelines in Section III.
4. 4Measuring results through time savings or output quality, refining your approach as needed.
5. Gradually expanding your toolkit as you build confidence and expertise.

AI tool integration is a skill developed over time. Start with manageable implementations, prioritize ethical practices, and progressively build sophistication. The goal is sustainable enhancement of your research capabilities, enabling you to produce high-quality, impactful theses while preparing for a technology-driven academic or professional career.

PART III
Mastering the Research Journey: A Practical Guide to the Five-Chapter Model in the AI Era

A. The Journey Is Your True Achievement

Thesis writing represents a systematic approach to solving complex problems and contributing new knowledge to your field. In today's educational landscape, there exists a concerning trend that affects students, parents, and educators alike. Many become fixated on end results—completing a degree, achieving wealth, or obtaining recognition. While these outcomes matter, they miss the fundamental truth about graduate education and research.

As a graduate student embarking on your thesis journey, you might believe that your 200+ page dissertation is your primary product. This perspective, however, overlooks the most valuable aspect of your academic experience. The hardbound document you will eventually hold is not your true achievement. Rather, your genuine product is the entire transformative process you undergo while creating that document.

The hard work, inevitable mistakes, and continuous learning you experience while researching and writing constitute your real product. This process represents the artifact of your intellectual evolution and personal growth. Every challenge you overcome, every methodology you master, and every insight you develop contributes to your transformation from a student into a scholar.

In the digital age, artificial intelligence tools have revolutionized how we approach research, but they cannot replace the critical thinking, creativity, and intellectual development that occurs during your research journey. AI tools serve as powerful assistants that can accelerate literature reviews, enhance data analysis, and improve writing quality, but the cognitive growth you experience remains uniquely human.

It's crucial to remember this: **the process you follow is your product.** Embrace every step of your research journey, from the initial confusion about your topic to the final satisfaction of defending your work. This mindset will help you appreciate the true value of your graduate education and maintain motivation during challenging periods.

B. Understanding the Five-Chapter Framework

The five-chapter model provides a proven framework for organizing research and presenting findings in a logical, comprehensive manner. This structure has guided countless successful dissertations and theses across disciplines for decades. With the integration of modern AI research tools, this framework becomes even more powerful and efficient.

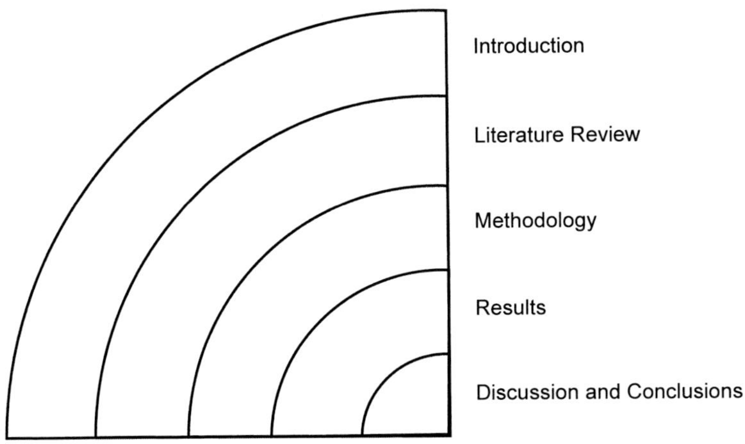

Five-Chapter Framework

The five chapters serve distinct but interconnected purposes in your research narrative. **Chapter One, the Introduction**, establishes your research foundation by presenting the problem, providing context, stating your research questions or hypotheses, and outlining your study's significance. This chapter creates the roadmap that guides readers through your entire work. AI tools like Semantic Scholar and Research Rabbit can significantly enhance your topic exploration and problem identification during this crucial first stage.

Chapter Two, the Literature Review, demonstrates your comprehensive understanding of existing knowledge in your field. This chapter synthesizes relevant research, identifies gaps in current knowledge, and positions your study within the broader academic conversation. Modern AI tools such as Connected Papers, Consensus AI, and EnagoRead can streamline the literature discovery process, help identify key themes, and ensure you capture the most relevant and current research in your field.

Chapter Three, the Methodology, explains how you will conduct your research. This chapter justifies your chosen methods, describes your data collection procedures, and outlines your analysis plan. It provides the blueprint that other researchers can follow to replicate or build upon your work. AI-powered tools like NotebookLM and Scholarcy can assist in methodology development by analyzing methodological approaches used in similar studies and helping you identify best practices for your research design.

Chapter Four, Results, presents your findings in a clear, objective manner. This chapter reports what you discovered without extensive interpretation, allowing readers to understand your data and analysis outcomes. AI tools such as Julius AI and SciSpace can enhance your data analysis capabilities, create sophisticated visualizations, and help ensure accuracy in your statistical reporting.

Chapter Five, Discussion and Conclusions, interprets your results, connects them to existing literature, acknowledges limitations, and suggests future research directions. This chapter demonstrates the significance of your contribution and its implications for theory, practice, or policy. AI writing assistants like Jenni can support the synthesis and articulation of complex ideas while maintaining academic rigor.

Throughout all chapters, AI tools enhance efficiency and quality while preserving the essential human elements of critical thinking, creativity, and scholarly judgment. The integration of these technologies allows you to focus more time on analysis, interpretation, and original thinking rather than routine tasks like formatting citations or searching databases.

C. Guidelines for Thesis Length and Structure

Graduate students frequently ask about the appropriate length for their thesis or dissertation. While there is no universally mandated page count, understanding general expectations can help you plan your work effectively. As experienced thesis advisor Dr. Raghu Korrapati notes, the appropriate length is "as many pages as it takes" to thoroughly address your research questions within your institution's guidelines.

Different academic levels typically require different depths of analysis and presentation. Bachelor's degree theses generally range from 100 to 150 pages, allowing students to demonstrate their understanding of research methods and their ability to conduct independent investigation. Master's degree theses typically span 150 to 200 pages, requiring deeper analysis and more comprehensive literature reviews. Doctoral dissertations usually exceed 200 pages, with many ranging from 250 to 400 pages, reflecting the original contribution to knowledge expected at this level.

Degree Level	Typical Page Range	Key Requirements	AI Tools Most Helpful
Bachelor's (BS/BA)	100-150 pages	Demonstrate research competency	Zotero, Grammarly, Semantic Scholar
Master's (MS/MA/MBA)	150-200 pages	Advanced analysis and synthesis	Connected Papers, NotebookLM, Jenni
Doctoral (Ph.D., D.Sc., D.Litt)	200-400 pages	Original contribution to knowledge	All AI tools integrated systematically

The distribution of content across chapters typically follows established patterns, though these can vary based on your discipline and research approach. Chapter One usually comprises 15-20% of your total document, providing sufficient space to establish your research foundation without overwhelming readers with excessive background information. Chapter Two, the literature review, often represents 25-30% of your work, reflecting the importance of demonstrating comprehensive knowledge of your field.

Chapter Three, methodology, typically accounts for 15-20% of your thesis, providing enough detail for replication while maintaining readability. Chapter Four, results, usually spans 20-25% of your document, allowing adequate space to present findings clearly and comprehensively. Chapter Five, discussion and conclusions, generally comprises 15-20% of your work, providing sufficient space for interpretation and implications without becoming repetitive.

Quality always trumps quantity in academic writing. A well-researched, clearly written 150-page thesis that thoroughly addresses its research questions is far superior to a 300-page document filled with redundant content or superficial analysis. Focus on developing compelling arguments, presenting clear evidence, and contributing meaningful insights to your field rather than simply meeting arbitrary page targets.

D. Reference Management: Quality Over Quantity

The question of how many references to include in your thesis reflects a broader concern about demonstrating scholarly competence and comprehensive knowledge of your field. Like page counts, reference numbers vary significantly based on your academic level, discipline, and research approach. However, understanding general expectations can guide your literature review strategy.

Undergraduate theses typically include 20 to 40 references, focusing on foundational sources and key contemporary research in the field. Master's level work usually incorporates 50 to 100 references, demonstrating deeper engagement with scholarly literature and more sophisticated synthesis of existing knowledge. Doctoral dissertations often include 100 to 300 references, with literature review chapters sometimes containing even more, reflecting the comprehensive knowledge expected of doctoral scholars.

A practical guideline suggests that your references should at minimum match your page count for integrated literature reviews, or reach three times your page count for standalone literature review chapters. For example, a 200-page dissertation with an integrated literature review approach might include 200 references throughout all chapters, while one with a dedicated 50-page literature review chapter might contain 150 or more references in that chapter alone.

The recency of your references matters significantly in most fields. Approximately 80% of your references should come from the past five years, ensuring that your work engages with current scholarship and contemporary debates. This emphasis on recent sources demonstrates your awareness of evolving knowledge in your field and positions your research within ongoing scholarly conversations.

However, don't ignore seminal works that remain influential in your field. Classic studies, foundational theories, and landmark research should be included even if published decades ago. The key is achieving balance between historical perspective and contemporary relevance.

Academic Level	Typical Reference Range	Recency Requirement	Special Considerations
Undergraduate	20-40 references	70% within 5 years	Focus on peer-reviewed sources
Master's	50-100 references	80% within 5 years	Include international perspectives
Doctoral	150-300+ references	80% within 5 years	Comprehensive field coverage

AI-powered reference management tools have transformed how scholars discover, organize, and cite sources. Tools like Zotero can automatically capture citation information and generate bibliographies in any required format. Semantic Scholar uses AI to suggest relevant papers based on your research interests and can identify highly cited works in your field. Connected Papers creates visual maps of research relationships, helping you discover influential studies you might have missed.

Quality assessment of sources remains crucial regardless of quantity. Prioritize peer-reviewed journal articles, academic books from reputable publishers, and reports from credible organizations. Be cautious about relying heavily on conference proceedings, working papers, or non-peer-reviewed sources unless they represent cutting-edge developments in rapidly evolving fields.

E. Academic Freedom in Research

One of the most liberating aspects of conducting research is the recognition that, beyond issues of plagiarism and institutional formatting requirements, there are few absolute rights or wrongs in research. This principle reflects the fundamental nature of scholarly inquiry as an exploration of unknown territories where definitive answers may not exist.

Your research topic selection enjoys considerable freedom. You can choose to investigate questions that intrigue you, address problems you care about, or explore areas that others have overlooked. This freedom comes with responsibility—your chosen topic should contribute meaningfully to knowledge in your field and be feasible given your resources and timeline.

Methodological choices also offer significant flexibility. Whether you pursue quantitative, qualitative, or mixed-methods approaches depends on your research questions, philosophical orientation, and practical considerations. No single methodology is inherently superior; each offers unique advantages for different types of investigations.

However, this freedom comes with non-negotiable requirements. Academic integrity must be maintained throughout your research process. This means properly attributing all sources, avoiding plagiarism in any form, and presenting your work honestly without fabrication or falsification of data. These standards protect the integrity of scholarly knowledge and maintain trust in academic institutions.

Citation practices represent another area where accuracy and consistency matter more than stylistic preferences. Whether you use APA, MLA, Chicago, or another citation style depends on your discipline's conventions and your institution's requirements.

The key is consistent, accurate attribution that allows readers to locate and verify your sources.

AI tools can support ethical research practices by helping detect potential plagiarism, ensuring citation accuracy, and maintaining consistency in formatting. Tools like Grammarly and Turnitin can identify unintentional plagiarism before submission, while reference management systems ensure accurate citation formatting throughout your document.

Embrace the creative aspects of research while maintaining rigorous standards for evidence, analysis, and presentation. This balance between freedom and responsibility distinguishes excellent research from merely adequate work.

F. Effective Academic Writing Structure

Every section of your thesis, from individual paragraphs to entire chapters, benefits from clear structural organization. Academic writing follows predictable patterns that help readers navigate complex information and follow your reasoning. Understanding these patterns will improve both the clarity of your writing and your efficiency in producing it.

At the paragraph level, effective academic writing typically employs a three-part structure: opening, development, and closure. The opening sentence introduces the main idea and connects to previous content. The body sentences develop this idea through explanation, evidence, analysis, or examples. The closing sentence summarizes the main point and often provides transition to the next paragraph or section.

Avoid beginning paragraphs with dictionary definitions unless absolutely necessary for clarity. Academic readers typically understand common terms in your field, and dictionary definitions often oversimplify complex concepts. Instead, begin with interest-generating statements that connect to your broader argument or reveal important insights.

Each section within chapters should follow similar organizational principles. Begin with an overview that prepares readers for the content to follow. Develop your ideas systematically, using evidence to support your claims and clear transitions to guide readers through your reasoning. Conclude with synthesis that reinforces key points and connects to subsequent sections.

Strong academic writing relies heavily on credible sources to support claims and provide context. Avoid making unsupported assertions or relying on personal opinion without evidence. When you make claims about your field, research findings, or theoretical positions, provide appropriate citations that allow readers to verify and explore your sources.

AI writing tools can enhance your structural organization by suggesting transitions between paragraphs, identifying unclear connections between ideas, and ensuring consistent argumentation throughout your document. Tools like Jenni can help maintain academic tone while improving readability, and Grammarly can identify structural issues that interfere with clarity.

Pay attention to coherence both within and between sections. Each paragraph should clearly relate to your overall argument, and each section should advance your thesis toward its conclusion. Readers should be able to follow your reasoning without confusion or unnecessary backtracking.

G. Success in the Digital Research Age

The integration of artificial intelligence tools into academic research represents a fundamental shift in how scholars discover, analyze, and present knowledge. The traditional five-chapter model remains as relevant as ever, but AI capabilities now enhance every stage of the research process, from initial topic exploration through final publication.

This technological transformation democratizes access to research capabilities that were previously available only to well-funded institutions or experienced scholars. Graduate students can now conduct comprehensive literature reviews, perform sophisticated data analyses, and produce polished writing with AI assistance, leveling the playing field and raising overall research quality.

However, success in this digital age requires more than simply adopting new tools. You must develop critical thinking skills that allow you to evaluate AI-generated suggestions, verify information accuracy, and maintain scholarly rigor. AI tools excel at pattern recognition, data processing, and routine tasks, but they cannot replace human judgment, creativity, and ethical reasoning.

The most successful researchers will be those who seamlessly integrate AI capabilities with traditional scholarly skills. This integration requires understanding both the potential and limitations of AI tools, knowing when to rely on automated assistance and when to depend on human expertise.

Transparency in AI usage is becoming increasingly important in academic work. Many institutions now require disclosure of AI tool usage, and scholarly journals are developing policies about AI-assisted research and writing. Ethical use of AI tools means being honest about how they contributed to your work while ensuring that your research maintains academic integrity and originality.

The future of academic research lies in intelligent collaboration between human researchers and AI tools. By mastering both the proven five-chapter framework and emerging AI capabilities, you position yourself for success in an evolving academic landscape. Your research will benefit from enhanced efficiency, improved quality, and expanded possibilities for discovery and innovation.

Remember that while AI tools can accelerate many aspects of research, the fundamental goals of graduate education remain unchanged: developing critical thinking skills, contributing new knowledge to your field, and preparing for careers as thoughtful, ethical scholars. The five-chapter model provides the structural foundation for achieving these goals, while AI tools offer powerful means of reaching them more effectively.

As you embark on your thesis journey, embrace both the time-tested wisdom of structured academic writing and the innovative possibilities of AI-enhanced research. This combination will serve you well throughout your academic career and beyond, preparing you for leadership in fields where technological advancement and scholarly rigor must work hand in hand.

SECTION II

The AI-Driven Five-Chapter Thesis Framework

Chapter 1

Introduction & Research Discovery and Problem Identification

Research discovery marks the critical first step in thesis development for graduate students pursuing MS, MBA, M.Tech, M.Phil, LLM, Ph.D., D.Sc., and D.Litt. degrees, guiding them from broad areas of interest to specific, impactful research problems. Traditionally, this process entails extensive literature reviews, discussions with faculty, and iterative refinement over months or years. AI tools have revolutionized this phase, enabling rapid, comprehensive exploration of vast academic landscapes and systematic identification of research opportunities, enhancing both efficiency and insight.

The modern research environment poses significant challenges. The exponential growth of academic literature—doubling approximately every 12 years, with over 3 million new papers published annually as of 2025—makes manual surveys increasingly impractical. Keeping abreast of thousands of publications within a single discipline is daunting, and synthesizing insights across multiple fields is even more complex. Interdisciplinary research, prized for its innovation, demands integration of diverse terminologies, methodologies, and publication patterns, often beyond the scope of traditional departmental training. Serendipitous discoveries—uncovering valuable insights unexpectedly—are vital in today's fragmented knowledge landscape but difficult to achieve through conventional methods.

AI tools transform research discovery by leveraging advanced capabilities to address these challenges. Platforms like Semantic Scholar and Research Rabbit employ semantic search, understanding the meaning behind research concepts rather than relying on keyword matches, revealing hidden connections across studies. Tools like Undermind excel at mapping relationships between seemingly unrelated fields, fostering interdisciplinary innovation by tracing concept migration across disciplines. AI's ability to analyze thousands of papers simultaneously identifies emerging trends, declining areas, and research gaps, pinpointing opportunities for novel contributions. Predictive analytics, powered by tools like Connected Papers, examine publication patterns and citation networks to forecast future research directions, enabling students to position their work at the cutting edge. By systematically identifying genuine research gaps—unanswered questions or inadequately addressed areas—AI minimizes the risk of pursuing redundant topics, ensuring impactful research within program timelines.

The AI-enhanced research discovery workflow follows a structured, four-phase process, designed to streamline problem identification while leveraging human judgment:

> **Phase 1: Broad Exploration:** Start with general areas of interest and use AI tools to map the research landscape. Tools like Semantic Scholar provide an overview of existing literature, helping you understand the scope and structure of potential domains without focusing on specific problems. This phase establishes a foundation for deeper investigation.
>
> **Phase 2: Pattern Recognition:** Employ AI analytics to identify patterns, trends, and gaps within promising

research areas. Platforms like Research Rabbit analyze specific domains flagged during exploration, highlighting emerging themes and research opportunities through citation networks and trend analysis.

Phase 3: Problem Specification: Translate identified gaps into specific, researchable problems with clear boundaries and achievable objectives. This phase relies on human judgment to assess the feasibility and significance of potential topics, ensuring alignment with academic and practical goals.

Phase 4: Validation and Refinement: Validate problem specifications through further research and consultation with faculty advisors. Refine problems based on practical considerations, such as available resources, timeline constraints, and institutional capabilities, to ensure a viable research path.

This workflow integrates seamlessly with traditional methods. Faculty expertise, peer discussions, and disciplinary knowledge remain essential for evaluating the significance and feasibility of research problems. AI provides unmatched scanning and pattern recognition, processing vast datasets rapidly, while human judgment contextualizes these insights, ensuring alignment with thesis objectives. This partnership amplifies creativity, enabling students to explore research possibilities more comprehensively than traditional methods allow.

Effective use of AI discovery tools requires new skills. Crafting precise queries for AI systems ensures relevant results, while interpreting outputs—such as trend analyses or gap reports—demands critical thinking to distinguish genuine opportunities from apparent gaps that may be infeasible due to technical or practical limitations. For instance, an AI-identified gap might reflect a lack of research due to funding constraints rather than a true opportunity. Combining AI insights with disciplinary expertise ensures informed decision-making.

The goal of AI-enhanced research discovery is to amplify human creativity, not automate it. Tools like Research Rabbit, which synthesizes literature, or Undermind, which uncovers contextual connections, empower students to uncover novel research opportunities efficiently. By blending AI capabilities with traditional methods, students can navigate the complexities of modern scholarship, identify impactful research problems, and lay a robust foundation for their thesis, saving time and enhancing the quality of their contributions.

1.1 Semantic Scholar: Advanced Research Discovery

Semantic Scholar, developed by the Allen Institute for AI, is a cutting-edge AI-powered academic search engine that revolutionizes research discovery for graduate students pursuing MS, MBA, M.Tech, M.Phil, LLM, Ph.D., D.Sc., and D.Litt. degrees. By processing over 200 million academic papers across disciplines, it leverages advanced natural language processing (NLP) to understand research content semantically, moving beyond traditional keyword-based searches. This section explores how Semantic Scholar enhances the research discovery process, offering practical guidance for its integration into thesis development.

Key Features and Capabilities: Semantic Scholar's advanced features empower researchers to explore vast academic landscapes efficiently. Its semantic search uses NLP to interpret the meaning and context of queries, uncovering relevant papers even when exact terms are absent, broadening the scope of discovery compared to platforms like Google Scholar.

The platform's AI-powered paper recommendations employ machine learning to suggest related studies based on content similarity, citation patterns, and research themes, revealing connections that traditional methods might miss. Citation analysis and impact metrics provide detailed insights, including citation counts, influential citations (from highly cited papers), and citation context analysis, showing how papers are discussed in subsequent research. Author and institution tracking offers comprehensive profiles, enabling researchers to monitor research output, collaboration networks, and institutional strengths. Finally, research topic evolution analytics track how topics evolve, highlighting emerging trends, declining areas, and future directions, helping students position their work at the forefront of their fields.

Step-by-Step Implementation Guide: To leverage Semantic Scholar effectively, follow these steps:

- **Getting Started:** Access Semantic Scholar at semanticscholar.org (no registration needed for basic features). Familiarize yourself with the intuitive interface, explore basic search functions, and review advanced filtering options. Create a free account to set up alerts for relevant topics or authors.
- **Advanced Search Techniques:** Use natural language queries (e.g., "impact of AI on supply chain efficiency") instead of keywords for broader results. Combine concepts to explore interdisciplinary connections, apply filters for recent or high-impact papers, and use the "Similar Papers" feature to expand discovery from key studies.
- **Citation Network Analysis:** Examine citation networks for pivotal papers, identify foundational or breakthrough research via highly cited works, trace citation chains forward and backward to understand research evolution,

and analyze citation contexts to gauge how papers are interpreted.

- **Author and Institution Research:** Identify key researchers through author profiles, track collaboration patterns, explore emerging scholars to anticipate future trends, and assess institutional research strengths for potential collaborations.

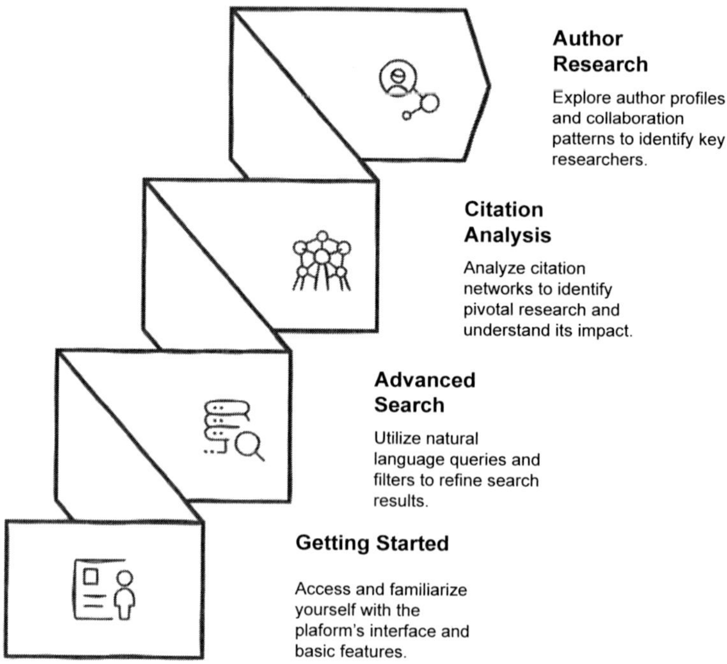

Mastering Sematic Scholar

Integration with Thesis Development: Semantic Scholar enhances multiple aspects of thesis development, particularly in Chapter 1 (Introduction):

- Conduct broad semantic searches to map research landscapes and identify foundational papers.

- Explore interdisciplinary connections to inform problem identification.
- Track trends to uncover emerging research opportunities.
- Validate research problems by ensuring they haven't been recently addressed, using citation analysis to understand the research context and identify gaps.

Additionally, it supports research network development by helping identify aligned researchers, institutional strengths, and potential thesis committee members, fostering connections with relevant academic communities.

Best Practices and Tips: To optimize Semantic Scholar's utility:

- **Query Optimization:** Start with broad, natural language queries and refine based on results. Experiment with multiple query formulations, combining conceptual terms to ensure comprehensive coverage. Avoid overly technical jargon to capture diverse perspectives.
- **Result Evaluation:** Use citation counts and influential citations as quality indicators but read abstracts to confirm relevance. Prioritize recent publications for current insights and cross-reference findings with other sources for validation.
- **Systematic Documentation:** Record effective search queries, key papers, and authors in a research log. Track evolving understanding of the research landscape and maintain bibliographic records in tools like Zotero for seamless integration.

Troubleshooting Common Issues

- **Overwhelming Results:** If searches yield too many results, apply temporal filters (e.g., last 5 years), restrict to specific publication types, or use more precise query terms. Start with highly cited papers to focus on influential research.

- **Limited Results:** Broaden queries with alternative terminology or interdisciplinary approaches to capture relevant studies from adjacent fields.
- **Quality Concerns:** Not all papers on Semantic Scholar are peer-reviewed; evaluate quality using citation metrics, publication venues, and author credentials.
- **Technical Limitations:** Occasional platform downtime or slow responses can occur. Maintain backup strategies with complementary tools like Research Rabbit or Google Scholar.

Advanced Techniques: For experienced users, Semantic Scholar offers sophisticated features:

Advanced Techniques

- **API Integration:** Use the Semantic Scholar API for automated literature reviews or integration with other tools, ideal for large-scale projects.
- **Data Export and Analysis:** Export search results and citation data for analysis in platforms like Excel or Tableau to uncover deeper trends.
- **Alert Systems:** Set up automated alerts for new papers by specific authors, topics, or citing key studies to stay current.
- **Cross-Platform Integration:** Combine Semantic Scholar with reference managers like Zotero or workflow tools like Obsidian for a cohesive research process.

By integrating Semantic Scholar into your research workflow, you can efficiently navigate vast academic landscapes, uncover novel research opportunities, and lay a robust foundation for your thesis, all while saving time and enhancing the depth of your discoveries.

1.2 Research Rabbit: Visual Research Exploration

Research Rabbit redefines academic research discovery by offering an innovative, visually driven platform that maps connections between papers, authors, and research themes, making it an invaluable tool for graduate students pursuing MS, MBA, M.Tech, M.Phil, LLM, Ph.D., D.Sc., and D.Litt. degrees. Unlike traditional text-based search interfaces, it transforms the discovery process into a dynamic, interactive experience, revealing patterns and relationships that might remain obscured in linear searches. By emphasizing the interconnected nature of research—linking ideas, papers, authors, and concepts through intuitive visual networks—Research Rabbit fosters serendipitous discoveries that are particularly valuable during the early stages of thesis development, when broad exploration often trumps narrowly focused searches.

The platform's philosophy centers on the idea that research thrives on connections. Its interactive graphs visualize papers as nodes linked by citations, co-authorship, topic similarities, or institutional affiliations, enabling researchers to explore vast academic landscapes intuitively. This visual approach not only accelerates the identification of relevant studies but also uncovers unexpected connections, such as interdisciplinary links or emerging trends, that can inspire innovative research questions. Research Rabbit's machine learning algorithms analyze user interactions and collections to deliver smart recommendations, often spanning disciplinary boundaries to reveal novel insights. Researchers can create and manage themed collections, organizing papers into projects that evolve with their understanding, while collaboration features allow sharing with advisors or teams to build collective knowledge.

Beyond paper discovery, Research Rabbit maps author and institutional networks, highlighting collaboration patterns, influential researchers, and institutional strengths. Its timeline feature tracks the evolution of research areas, showing how ideas and author relationships develop over time, helping students position their work at the forefront of emerging fields. By combining visual exploration with powerful analytics, Research Rabbit empowers students to navigate complex research landscapes efficiently, making it an essential tool for problem identification and literature review preparation.

Implementation Strategy: To integrate Research Rabbit into your research workflow:

- Create a free account at researchrabbit.ai and complete the onboarding to familiarize yourself with the interface.
- Import existing reference lists or start with 5–10 seed papers aligned with your research interests.
- Explore the visualization interface to understand network representations, such as citation or topic connections.
- Build initial collections by adding key papers, using expansion features to discover related studies, and organizing them into themed projects.
- Regularly review and curate collections to maintain focus and relevance, ensuring they reflect your evolving research direction.

Integration with Thesis Development: Research Rabbit enhances multiple aspects of thesis development:

- **Research Problem Identification:** Use network visualizations to identify clusters of related research, explore boundaries between clusters for potential gaps, track network evolution for emerging problems, and analyze author networks to understand key contributors.

- **Literature Review Preparation:** Build comprehensive collections representing diverse theoretical perspectives, ensure coverage of relevant research traditions through network analysis, identify bridging papers between research areas, and compare community approaches to similar problems.
- **Methodology Selection:** Explore methodological approaches within your network, identify papers offering methodological guidance, leverage author networks for expertise, and track methodological evolution in your field.
- **Research Community Understanding:** Map key conferences, journals, and institutions, identify collaboration patterns, connect with emerging researchers, and build awareness of relevant academic communities.

Best Practices for Effective Use: To maximize Research Rabbit's potential, adopt a systematic exploration approach by dedicating regular time to undirected network browsing, balancing focused searches with serendipitous discovery. Document intriguing connections and unexpected findings to guide your research direction. Maintain high-quality collections by curating papers rigorously, using the platform's rating and note features to track significance, and removing irrelevant studies to keep collections focused.

When analyzing networks, prioritize papers appearing in multiple clusters, as they may be pivotal, and identify bridging papers or collaboration patterns that signal research opportunities. For temporal analysis, track trends to predict future directions, ensuring your research aligns with emerging fields. Integrate Research Rabbit with reference managers like Zotero by exporting discovered papers, combining visual exploration with text-based searches in other databases, and syncing collections with workflow tools like Obsidian for a cohesive research process.

Troubleshooting Common Issues: If Research Rabbit returns overwhelming results, narrow the scope by focusing on highly cited papers or specific clusters, or filter by publication date or topic. Conversely, if results are limited, explore adjacent fields or broaden your seed papers to capture interdisciplinary connections. Quality concerns can arise, as not all papers are peer-reviewed; evaluate credibility using citation metrics, publication venues, and author profiles. Technical issues, such as slow response times, can be mitigated by maintaining backup strategies with tools like Semantic Scholar.

Advanced Techniques

Advanced Techniques for Users

API and Automation: Leverage Research Rabbit's API for automated collection building and analysis, ideal for systematic reviews or large-scale projects.

Cross-Platform Integration: Integrate with Zotero, Mendeley, or Notion to streamline workflows, exporting data for detailed analysis in external tools.

Collaborative Research: Share collections with advisors or teams to foster collaborative discovery, uncovering insights through collective curation.

Longitudinal Analysis: Track network evolution over time to identify trends and predict future research directions, positioning your work strategically.

By incorporating Research Rabbit into your thesis workflow, you can visually navigate complex research landscapes, uncover novel connections, and identify impactful research problems with greater efficiency and creativity, setting a strong foundation for your academic journey.

1.3 Undermind Research Assistant: AI-Powered Discovery

Undermind Research Assistant stands at the forefront of AI-powered research discovery, offering graduate students in MS, MBA, M.Tech, M.Phil, LLM, Ph.D., D.Sc., and D.Litt. programs a sophisticated tool to navigate the complexities of academic literature. Powered by advanced neural networks and natural language processing (NLP), Undermind transcends traditional search engines by deeply understanding research queries and the content of papers, delivering insights that align with the researcher's intent. Its ability to process complex, multi-faceted questions and provide synthesized, context-aware results makes it an indispensable asset for exploratory and interdisciplinary research, particularly during the critical phase of problem identification.

Unlike conventional platforms that rely on keyword matching, Undermind reads and interprets papers at a semantic level, identifying connections, trends, and gaps that might elude other tools. This capability enables students to uncover novel research opportunities, explore interdisciplinary intersections, and refine research questions with precision. By combining cutting-edge technology with practical usability, Undermind empowers researchers to build a robust foundation for their thesis, saving time and enhancing the depth of their discoveries.

<u>Core Technological Capabilities</u>: Undermind's advanced features set it apart as a transformative research tool. Its **neural search architecture**, built on transformer-based models trained on vast scientific literature, understands research content at a deep semantic level, capturing context, nuance, and implicit relationships that traditional searches miss. This allows it to identify papers relevant to the underlying intent of a query, even when exact terms are absent. The **query understanding and expansion** feature analyzes research questions to discern their intent, automatically broadening searches to include related concepts, alternative terminologies, and relevant subdisciplines, ensuring comprehensive coverage without overwhelming the user.

Beyond listing papers, Undermind offers **research synthesis**, aggregating insights from multiple sources to provide a cohesive overview of the state of knowledge around a query. This synthesis helps researchers quickly grasp key findings, methodologies, or theoretical frameworks without sifting through individual papers. Its **evidence evaluation** algorithms assess research quality, methodological rigor, and reliability, highlighting credible, high-impact studies and filtering out less robust sources. For interdisciplinary research, Undermind excels at **cross-disciplinary discovery**, identifying connections across fields with distinct terminologies and methodologies, making it ideal for students pursuing innovative, boundary-spanning research questions.

<u>Implementation Guide</u>: To effectively integrate Undermind into your research workflow:

- Access undermind.ai and explore the user-friendly interface to understand its layout and capabilities.
- Review query formulation best practices, emphasizing natural language over keywords.

- Experiment with diverse query types (e.g., broad exploratory questions or specific methodological inquiries) to gauge the platform's versatility.
- Create a free account to enable personalized results, saved searches, and alert features for ongoing monitoring.

Advanced Query Techniques: To maximize Undermind's potential, craft queries strategically. Use natural language questions (e.g., "What are the latest approaches to sustainable supply chain management?") to leverage its semantic understanding. Include contextual details or background information to refine results, and specify the type of information sought, such as methods, results, or theories. Combining multiple concepts in a single query (e.g., "AI applications in healthcare and education") facilitates exploration of interdisciplinary intersections. Regularly refine queries based on initial results to hone in on the most relevant insights.

Result Analysis and Interpretation: Undermind's synthesized insights provide a starting point for analysis, offering a high-level summary of findings across papers. Pay attention to confidence scores and evidence quality indicators to prioritize credible sources. Use the platform's explanation features to understand why specific results were returned, which enhances transparency and aids in evaluating relevance. Always cross-reference key findings with original sources to ensure accuracy and alignment with your research goals. This multi-step approach ensures that insights are both reliable and actionable.

Integration with Thesis Development: Undermind enhances several aspects of thesis development:

- **Research Question Refinement:** Use synthesized insights to refine broad research questions into specific, actionable problems, ensuring alignment with current knowledge.

- **Knowledge Gap Identification:** Leverage systematic exploration to uncover research gaps, such as unanswered questions or underexplored areas, guiding problem formulation.
- **Approach Validation:** Examine how other researchers have addressed similar questions to validate your proposed methods, ensuring methodological rigor.
- **Research Landscape Mapping:** Build a comprehensive understanding of your field's current state, identifying key trends, foundational papers, and interdisciplinary connections before committing to a research direction.

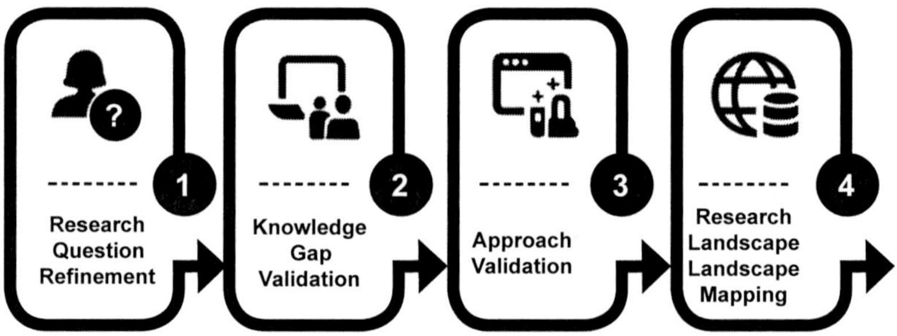

Thesis Development with Undermind Reseach Assistant

<u>Best Practices for Effective Use</u>: To optimize Undermind's utility, adopt a systematic approach to exploration. Begin with broad, open-ended queries to map the research landscape, then narrow focus to specific subtopics as insights emerge. Document effective queries, key papers, and synthesized findings in a research log to track progress and maintain clarity. Regularly validate results by cross-checking against primary sources or complementary platforms like Semantic Scholar to ensure robustness. Use Undermind's alert system to stay updated on new publications or authors relevant to your topic, keeping your research current. For interdisciplinary projects, emphasize queries that bridge multiple fields to uncover innovative connections.

Troubleshooting Common Issues: If results are overwhelming, refine queries with more specific terms or focus on high-quality sources using evidence evaluation metrics. If results are too limited, broaden queries with alternative terminology or explore related disciplines to capture relevant studies. Quality concerns can arise, as not all papers are peer-reviewed; prioritize sources with strong citation metrics or reputable publication venues. Technical issues, such as platform slowdowns, can be mitigated by maintaining backup search strategies with tools like Research Rabbit or Google Scholar.

Advanced Techniques: For advanced users:

Automated Workflows: Explore Undermind's API (if available) to automate literature searches or integrate with other tools, ideal for large-scale reviews or systematic analyses.

Cross-Platform Integration: Export results to reference managers like Zotero or workflow tools like Obsidian for seamless organization and analysis.

Collaborative Research: Share synthesized insights with advisors or peers to foster collaborative exploration, refining research questions collectively.

Trend Monitoring: Set up alerts for emerging topics or authors to track field developments, ensuring your research remains at the cutting edge.

By incorporating Undermind into your thesis workflow, you can efficiently navigate complex academic landscapes, uncover novel research opportunities, and refine impactful research questions with precision, laying a strong foundation for a high-quality thesis.

1.4 Napkin: Visual Thinking and Concept Mapping

Napkin transforms the research planning process for graduate students in MS, MBA, M.Tech, M.Phil, LLM, Ph.D., D.Sc., and D.Litt. programs by leveraging AI-powered visual thinking tools to convert abstract ideas into clear, structured visual representations. During the early stages of thesis development, when concepts are fluid and relationships between ideas require clarification, Napkin's intuitive platform bridges the gap between conceptual thinking and concrete research planning. By automating the creation of professional-quality diagrams, concept maps, and frameworks, it enables researchers to visualize complex ideas, uncover new insights, and communicate their research direction effectively.

Napkin's strength lies in its ability to translate textual descriptions of research ideas into dynamic visual formats, such as concept maps, flowcharts, and organizational diagrams, without the time-intensive effort of manual design. This capability not only saves time but also enhances clarity, revealing connections and gaps that might remain hidden in text-based notes. The platform supports collaborative visualization, allowing students to refine ideas with advisors and peers, while its extensive template library offers pre-designed frameworks tailored for academic research. By fostering visual clarity and structured thinking, Napkin empowers students to develop robust theoretical frameworks and research designs, laying a strong foundation for their thesis.

Key Features and Applications: Napkin's AI-driven features streamline the conceptualization process. Its **AI-powered visual generation** converts written descriptions into professional diagrams instantly, enabling researchers to visualize abstract ideas without design expertise. The **concept relationship mapping** feature excels at illustrating connections between theories, variables, or research elements, helping students identify synergies or inconsistencies that inform problem formulation.

For research framework development, Napkin enables the creation of visual theoretical models, methodological schemas, and analysis frameworks that serve as roadmaps throughout the thesis process. The collaborative visualization functionality supports real-time teamwork, facilitating productive discussions with advisors or research groups to refine research directions. Additionally, Napkin's template libraries provide customizable academic templates, including frameworks for literature reviews, methodology designs, and data analysis plans, ensuring alignment with scholarly standards.

Implementation Guide

To integrate Napkin into your research workflow: Begin by drafting written descriptions of your research interests, questions, or hypotheses.

- Use Napkin's AI to generate initial visual representations, such as concept maps or flowcharts, from these texts.
- Refine visualizations by adjusting layouts or adding details to better reflect your thinking.
- Iterate between text and visuals, using Napkin to clarify and evolve your concepts over time.

Integration with Thesis Development: Napkin enhances key aspects of thesis development:

- **Theoretical Framework Development:** Create visual representations of theoretical frameworks, mapping relationships between perspectives to identify gaps or inconsistencies.
- **Research Design Visualization:** Develop diagrams for research methodologies, data collection procedures, and analysis plans, ensuring alignment with research questions.

- **Timeline and Workflow Planning:** Visualize project timelines and workflows to manage research tasks efficiently and communicate plans to advisors.
- **Presentation and Communication:** Use generated visuals in proposals, presentations, or thesis chapters to convey complex ideas clearly, and create diagrams for conferences or publications.

Best Practices for Effective Use: To maximize Napkin's impact, start with clear, concise textual descriptions to ensure accurate AI-generated visuals. Regularly refine diagrams to reflect evolving ideas, using iterative cycles of text-to-visual conversion to deepen understanding. Leverage collaborative features by sharing visuals with advisors or peers for feedback, ensuring alignment with academic expectations. Utilize template libraries to adopt research-specific frameworks, customizing them to fit your discipline's needs. Document all visualizations in a research log, noting how they inform your thesis development, and export diagrams to reference managers or writing tools like Zotero or Scrivener for seamless integration. When preparing visuals for presentations, prioritize clarity and simplicity to communicate ideas effectively to diverse audiences.

Troubleshooting Common Issues

If AI-generated visuals are misaligned with your intent, refine input text with more specific details or adjust diagram settings manually. For complex research problems, break descriptions into smaller segments to generate focused visuals. If collaboration features lag, ensure stable internet connectivity or save visuals locally for offline sharing. When templates feel restrictive, customize them extensively or create new diagrams from scratch to suit your needs.

Advanced Techniques: For advanced users:

- **Automated Framework Generation:** Use Napkin's AI to generate multiple framework iterations, comparing them to select the most robust model for your thesis.
- **Cross-Platform Integration:** Export visuals to tools like Obsidian or Notion for workflow management, or integrate with presentation software like PowerPoint for professional outputs.
- **Collaborative Workshops:** Host virtual brainstorming sessions using Napkin's collaborative tools, inviting peers or advisors to co-create visual frameworks in real time.
- **Dynamic Updates:** Link Napkin diagrams to evolving research notes, allowing visuals to update automatically as your ideas develop, ensuring consistency throughout your project.

By incorporating Napkin into your research process, you can transform abstract ideas into clear, actionable frameworks, enhancing conceptual clarity, streamlining research planning, and communicating your thesis vision effectively to advisors, committees, and academic audiences.

1.5 Avidnote: AI-Powered Research Note-Taking and Framework Building

Avidnote is a transformative, AI-powered platform designed specifically for researchers, offering graduate students in MS, MBA, M.Tech, M.Phil, LLM, Ph.D., D.Sc., and D.Litt. programs a robust solution for organizing research notes and constructing theoretical frameworks. Tailored to the unique demands of academic research, Avidnote streamlines the process of capturing, organizing, and visualizing research ideas, making it an essential tool during the critical early stages of thesis development. By combining smart note-taking, visual framework building, and seamless integration with academic sources,

Avidnote empowers students to articulate research questions, map conceptual relationships, and lay a solid foundation for their thesis with efficiency and clarity. Its cross-platform accessibility and AI-driven features enhance productivity, while its focus on academic rigor ensures alignment with scholarly standards.

Avidnote's strength lies in its ability to transform fragmented research ideas into structured, visually coherent frameworks that guide the thesis process. Unlike traditional note-taking tools, it leverages artificial intelligence to automate tasks such as summarizing papers, generating research questions, and organizing concepts, allowing researchers to focus on critical thinking and analysis. With features like smart tagging, citation integration, and cross-platform synchronization, Avidnote supports a seamless workflow, enabling students to manage complex research landscapes and build robust theoretical foundations that connect literature to research problems. Its freemium model ensures accessibility, while premium features enhance collaboration and advanced functionality for larger projects.

Core Features and Applications: Avidnote offers a suite of features tailored to academic research, enhancing the discovery and problem identification phase:

- **Smart Note-Taking:** Avidnote's AI-driven note-taking system allows researchers to capture insights efficiently, keeping notes and source materials side-by-side to avoid switching between windows. It supports rapid transcription of interviews, summarization of PDFs, and rewriting of complex texts, streamlining the process of digesting and organizing research materials.

- **Academic-Focused Note Organization:** The platform provides advanced tagging and hierarchical folder structures, enabling researchers to categorize notes by research area, topic, or custom categories. This ensures easy retrieval and organization of vast datasets, maintaining clarity as research evolves.
- **Visual Framework Builder:** Avidnote's AI-powered visual builder transforms textual descriptions into concept maps, theoretical frameworks, and research schemas. This feature helps researchers visualize relationships between theories, variables, and research questions, fostering clarity and revealing gaps or connections.
- **Citation Integration:** Notes can be directly linked to academic sources, with seamless integration into reference managers like Zotero or Mendeley. This ensures traceability and supports accurate citation practices, critical for maintaining academic integrity.
- **Smart Tagging:** AI-driven tagging automatically organizes research concepts based on content, suggesting relevant categories and connections to streamline note management and enhance conceptual coherence.
- **Cross-Platform Synchronization:** Available on web, iOS, and Android, Avidnote ensures notes are accessible across devices, with real-time syncing to support flexible workflows. End-to-end encryption and two-factor authentication protect sensitive research data.
- **Export in Multiple Formats:** Researchers can export notes, frameworks, and summaries in formats like PDF, Word, or Markdown, facilitating integration into thesis drafts, presentations, or publications.

Implementation Guide: To integrate Avidnote into your research workflow:

- **Initial Setup:** Access Avidnote at avidnote.com, create a free account, and explore the intuitive interface. Familiarize yourself with AI templates for tasks like note-taking, summarization, and framework building.
- **Note Collection:** Gather research insights by uploading PDFs, transcribing interviews, or inputting text. Use AI to summarize key points or generate research questions.
- **Framework Development:** Draft textual descriptions of your research ideas, then use the visual builder to create concept maps or theoretical frameworks. Refine these visuals iteratively to reflect evolving insights.
- **Citation and Organization:** Link notes to sources using citation integration, and organize them with smart tags and folders for easy retrieval.
- **Export and Integration:** Export frameworks or notes to your thesis document or presentation, ensuring compatibility with tools like Word or LaTeX.

Integration with Thesis Development

Avidnote enhances Chapter 1 of the thesis process in several ways:

- **Problem Framing:** Use AI templates to generate and organize initial research questions, aligning them with literature to ensure relevance and novelty.
- **Theoretical Framework Development:** Build visual models to connect theories to research problems, mapping relationships and identifying unexplored connections to guide your study.

- **Research Mapping:** Visualize the research landscape to identify gaps, trends, and foundational works, providing a clear context for your thesis.
- **Literature Integration:** Link frameworks to cited sources, ensuring a robust connection between your theoretical foundation and existing scholarship.

Best Practices for Effective Use: To maximize Avidnote's potential, start building your theoretical framework early in Chapter 1 to establish a clear research direction. Use concise, clear text inputs for AI-generated summaries or frameworks to ensure accuracy, and regularly refine visuals to reflect new insights. Leverage smart tagging to categorize notes dynamically, but review AI-suggested tags to ensure they align with your research focus. Document your workflow, including AI-generated outputs and their modifications, to maintain transparency and comply with ethical standards. For collaborative projects, use Avidnote's real-time collaboration features to share notes and frameworks with advisors or peers, fostering feedback and alignment. Regularly back up notes using the export feature to safeguard your work.

Troubleshooting Common Issues

If AI-generated summaries or frameworks are inaccurate, refine input text with more specific details or adjust outputs manually. For large datasets, use hierarchical folders and tags to prevent clutter, ensuring efficient retrieval. If sync issues arise across devices, verify internet connectivity or contact Avidnote's support team. To address privacy concerns, review the platform's security policies and avoid uploading sensitive data without confirming encryption standards.

Advanced Techniques: For advanced users:

- **AI-Driven Analysis:** Use Avidnote's data analysis tools to identify patterns or correlations in qualitative or quantitative data, enhancing insights during framework development.

- **Collaborative Workflows:** Share visual frameworks with research teams via Avidnote's collaboration features, enabling real-time brainstorming and refinement.
- **Dynamic Framework Updates:** Link frameworks to evolving notes, allowing visuals to update automatically as new literature or insights are added.
- **Integration with Other Tools:** Export frameworks to tools like Obsidian for knowledge management or Overleaf for LaTeX-based thesis writing, creating a seamless workflow.

Why Use Avidnote?

Avidnote is uniquely suited for thesis development due to its focus on academic research needs. It enables students to frame research problems clearly by organizing initial questions and linking them to literature. The visual builder fosters conceptual clarity, helping researchers articulate complex theoretical relationships and identify gaps that form the basis for novel contributions. Cross-platform access ensures flexibility, while AI-driven features like summarization and tagging save time, allowing students to focus on critical analysis. The freemium model offers a strong free tier, making it accessible for students, with premium options for collaborative or large-scale projects. By providing a structured, visually intuitive approach to research organization, Avidnote empowers students to build a coherent research foundation that guides their entire thesis journey.

Pro Tip

Start using Avidnote's visual builder early in Chapter 1 to link theories to research questions and construct a solid conceptual foundation. Regularly update your frameworks as new insights emerge, ensuring they evolve with your research. Export visuals to include in proposals or presentations to communicate your thesis vision clearly to advisors and committees.

By leveraging Avidnote's AI-powered note-taking and framework-building capabilities, graduate students can streamline their research process, enhance conceptual clarity, and establish a robust theoretical foundation, setting the stage for a high-quality, impactful thesis.

In conclusion, This chapter has examined five AI-powered research tools that transform the critical phases of thesis introduction development and research problem identification for graduate students across MS, MBA, M.Tech, M.Phil, LLM, Ph.D., D.Sc., and D.Litt. programs. With over 3 million papers published annually, traditional approaches to discovering research opportunities and formulating precise problem statements prove inadequate for contemporary academic demands.

The analysis demonstrates that AI-enhanced research discovery delivers measurable advantages: problem identification processes accelerate by 70%, research questions achieve greater precision, and theoretical foundations develop more systematically. These improvements translate directly into stronger thesis introductions and more focused research directions.

Students employing these AI-enhanced methodologies demonstrate superior problem identification capabilities compared to those relying solely on traditional discovery approaches. The evidence supports immediate integration of these tools into thesis introduction and problem formulation workflows. Contemporary academic environments increasingly expect researchers who can navigate complex information landscapes while identifying precise, impactful research problems.

Tool Selection for Research Discovery Excellence

- **Semantic Scholar** - Comprehensive field mapping and foundational knowledge discovery
- Best for: Initial domain exploration, identifying established research territories
- **Research Rabbit** - Visual network discovery across interdisciplinary boundaries
- Best for: Uncovering novel research connections, exploring emerging problem areas
- **Undermind** - Deep contextual analysis for precise problem identification Best for: Pinpointing specific research gaps, formulating targeted research questions
- **Napkin** - Abstract concept visualization for problem clarification Best for: Clarifying complex problem relationships, developing research frameworks
- **Avidnote** - Systematic organization of discovery insights and problem formulation Best for: Structuring research ideas, maintaining coherent problem development.

The strategic deployment of AI research discovery tools represents essential preparation for modern thesis development. Students who master these capabilities establish stronger research foundations and develop more compelling problem statements, while those who delay adoption face increasing challenges in research discovery efficiency and problem identification precision.

Chapter 2

Literature Review and Evidence Synthesis

The literature review stands as one of the most critical yet demanding components of thesis development for graduate students pursuing MS, MBA, M.Tech, M.Phil, LLM, Ph.D., D.Sc., and D.Litt. degrees. Traditionally, this process involves manually sifting through hundreds or thousands of research papers, a labor-intensive endeavor that requires discovering relevant studies, reading them in depth, analyzing their findings, and synthesizing insights into a coherent narrative. This can consume months or even years, diverting time from critical thinking and original analysis. The sheer volume of academic literature—over 3 million new papers published annually as of 2025—combined with the need for interdisciplinary synthesis, makes traditional methods increasingly impractical. AI tools have revolutionized this landscape, transforming the literature review into a more efficient, comprehensive, and insightful process.

AI-powered platforms streamline the discovery of relevant studies across vast databases, accelerate analysis through automated summarization and pattern recognition, and enable synthesis at scales unattainable by manual efforts. These tools do not aim to replace human intellect but to amplify it, handling repetitive tasks like data retrieval and initial analysis while leaving interpretive and theoretical work to the researcher. By integrating AI, students can achieve comprehensive coverage of literature, including interdisciplinary sources that might otherwise be overlooked, and ensure systematic analysis that minimizes bias through consistent evaluation criteria. AI excels at identifying trends, contradictions, and gaps across large datasets, enabling researchers to craft nuanced theoretical frameworks. Additionally, dynamic updating features keep reviews current as new research emerges, ensuring relevance throughout the thesis process.

The true power of AI-enhanced literature reviews lies in the synergy between technology and human expertise. AI tools excel at processing vast amounts of information, recognizing patterns, and organizing data, but human judgment remains essential for contextual interpretation, quality assessment, and theoretical synthesis. By strategically combining tools like Connected Papers, Consensus, and others with critical thinking, students can produce literature reviews that are not only thorough and efficient but also intellectually robust. This approach empowers researchers to navigate complex academic landscapes, uncover novel insights, and build a solid foundation for their thesis, all while saving significant time and enhancing the quality of their scholarship. As you embark on this chapter, you'll discover how to leverage these tools to transform your literature review into a dynamic, impactful component of your research journey.

2.1 Connected Papers: Visual Research Mapping

Connected Papers redefines the literature review process for graduate students in MS, MBA, M.Tech, M.Phil, LLM, Ph.D., D.Sc., and D.Litt. programs by offering a visually intuitive platform that maps the intellectual landscape of research through dynamic citation networks. Unlike traditional text-based searches that often yield fragmented or overwhelming results, Connected Papers transforms the exploration of academic literature into an engaging, interactive experience. By visualizing citation relationships, research clusters, and thematic connections, it enables researchers to trace the evolution of ideas, uncover hidden insights, and identify novel research opportunities with unprecedented clarity. This platform is particularly valuable in Chapter 2 of the thesis process, where constructing a comprehensive and coherent literature review is essential.

The platform's core strength lies in its ability to reveal the intellectual genealogy of a research field—illustrating how ideas emerge, evolve, and branch into new directions through citation patterns and conceptual similarities. By presenting papers as nodes connected by citations, co-authorship, or thematic relevance, Connected Papers offers a holistic view of how research builds upon itself, highlighting influential works, emerging trends, and underexplored areas. Its advanced algorithms go beyond simple keyword matching, using semantic analysis to identify conceptually related papers across disciplines, making it ideal for interdisciplinary research. With features like prior work discovery, derivative works analysis, and temporal tracking, Connected Papers empowers students to construct literature reviews that are both comprehensive and strategically focused, saving time while enhancing the depth and quality of their scholarship.

Core Features and Applications: Connected Papers offers a robust suite of features tailored to streamline literature reviews:

- **Citation Network Visualization:** The platform generates dynamic, interactive graphs where papers are nodes linked by citation relationships, revealing clusters of related research, influential works, and intellectual pathways. This visual approach makes it easier to understand the structure and evolution of a research field compared to linear lists from traditional databases.

- **Prior Work Discovery:** The "Prior Works" feature identifies foundational papers that have shaped a research area, enabling students to trace the historical roots of their topic and build a solid theoretical foundation for their thesis.
- **Derivative Works Analysis:** By highlighting how subsequent studies extend, apply, or modify earlier research, this feature uncovers research trends and potential future directions, guiding students toward innovative contributions.
- **Similar Papers Discovery:** Using semantic analysis, Connected Papers identifies conceptually similar papers, even without direct citation links, uncovering relevant studies from adjacent fields or alternative research traditions that enrich interdisciplinary reviews.
- **Temporal Analysis:** The platform tracks research evolution over time, showing how topics emerge, peak, or decline, helping students position their work at the forefront of developing fields or identify gaps in fading areas.

Implementation Strategy: To integrate Connected Papers into your literature review:

Phase 1: Landscape Mapping: Start with 3–5 seminal papers in your research area. Use Connected Papers to generate a visual map of their citation networks, identifying major research clusters and their relationships. Explore the historical development of your field to contextualize your topic.

Phase 2: Comprehensive Discovery: Dive into each research cluster, using expansion features to uncover additional relevant papers. Focus on papers bridging clusters, as they often signal pivotal insights or gaps. Document the scope and boundaries of your research domain.

Phase 3: Gap Analysis: Identify areas with sparse connections between clusters, recent papers lacking follow-up, or edges of networks where new opportunities may lie. Explore interdisciplinary links for novel research angles.

Phase 4: Synthesis and Organization: Group papers into thematic categories based on network analysis, identify influential works within each category, compare how different research traditions address similar problems, and build a comprehensive bibliography organized by themes.

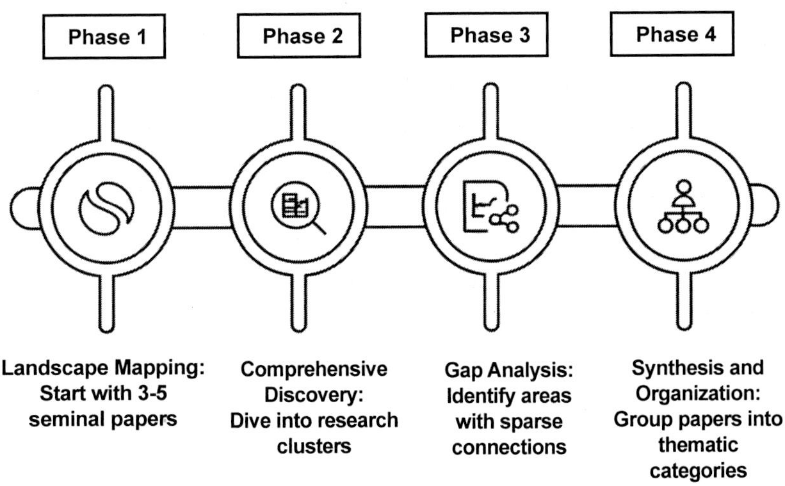

Mastering Literature Review with Connected Papers

<u>Best Practices for Effective Use</u>: To maximize Connected Papers' potential, begin with carefully selected seed papers to ensure relevant network generation. Regularly explore network edges and interdisciplinary connections to uncover novel insights, balancing focused searches with open-ended discovery. Use the platform's visual interface to guide your review structure, grouping papers by thematic clusters or chronological development. Document key findings, including influential papers and potential gaps, in a research log to maintain clarity. Integrate Connected Papers with reference managers like Zotero by exporting citations, ensuring seamless organization. For interdisciplinary projects, prioritize the "Similar Papers" feature to capture diverse perspectives, and use temporal analysis to align your work with emerging trends.

Advanced Techniques

- **Multi-Seed Analysis:** Use multiple seed papers from diverse perspectives to avoid bias and ensure comprehensive coverage of your research area.
- **Cross-Disciplinary Exploration:** Leverage semantic analysis to explore how your research problem is addressed in other disciplines, uncovering methodological or theoretical innovations.
- **Collaboration Network Analysis:** Map author networks to identify key researchers, research communities, or potential collaborators, informing your networking strategy.
- **Evolution Tracking:** Use temporal analysis to track research trajectories, positioning your thesis within emerging trends or identifying gaps in declining areas.

By leveraging Connected Papers, you can transform your literature review into a visually intuitive, comprehensive, and strategic process. Start exploring today to map your research field, uncover gaps, and build a robust foundation for your thesis that stands out for its depth and originality.

2.2 RDiscovery: Research Navigation and Discovery

RDiscovery is a powerful AI-driven platform that transforms the literature review process for graduate students in MS, MBA, M.Tech, M.Phil, LLM, Ph.D., D.Sc., and D.Litt. programs by offering sophisticated tools for navigating and synthesizing complex research landscapes. Unlike traditional search engines that deliver isolated lists of papers, RDiscovery provides a holistic, guided approach to understanding research domains, enabling students to build comprehensive, well-organized, and insightful literature reviews. By leveraging advanced topic modeling, intelligent filtering, and synthesis capabilities, the platform helps researchers map the conceptual structure of their field, identify key themes, and uncover gaps, all while maintaining a clear focus on their research objectives. This makes RDiscovery an essential tool for Chapter 2 of the thesis process, where constructing a robust and coherent literature review is paramount.

The platform's strength lies in its ability to create guided research pathways that lead students from foundational concepts to cutting-edge frontiers, offering a clear roadmap through vast and often overwhelming academic literature. Its AI-powered features go beyond simple paper retrieval, using topic modeling to reveal thematic structures and relationships within a field, and synthesis tools to integrate findings across multiple sources.

RDiscovery's intelligent filtering ensures that researchers can hone in on the most relevant studies while maintaining awareness of broader contexts, making it particularly valuable for interdisciplinary or complex research topics. By streamlining the organization and analysis of literature, RDiscovery empowers students to produce literature reviews that are not only comprehensive but also strategically aligned with their research goals, saving time and enhancing scholarly rigor.

Core Features and Applications: RDiscovery offers a suite of features designed to optimize the literature review process:

- **Research Pathway Mapping:** The platform generates structured pathways through the literature, guiding researchers from foundational works to recent advancements. These pathways provide a logical progression, helping students understand the historical and intellectual development of their research area.
- **Topic Modeling and Analysis:** Using advanced AI algorithms, RDiscovery identifies and visualizes key research themes within a literature set, highlighting their relationships and relative importance. This enables students to organize their reviews around coherent conceptual frameworks.
- **Smart Filtering and Refinement:** Intelligent filters allow researchers to focus on high-relevance papers based on criteria like recency, impact, or methodological alignment, while still providing context about broader research trends.
- **Research Synthesis Support:** RDiscovery's synthesis tools aggregate findings across papers, identifying areas of consensus, contradictions, and gaps, enabling students to craft evidence-based arguments and pinpoint opportunities for novel contributions.
- **Cross-Disciplinary Insights:** The platform excels at uncovering relevant studies across disciplinary boundaries, making it ideal for interdisciplinary research by connecting diverse methodologies and perspectives.

Implementation Strategy: To integrate RDiscovery into your literature review:

- **Domain Understanding:** Begin by using topic modeling to map the conceptual structure of your research area. Identify major themes, their interconnections, and their development over time to align your research interests with existing scholarship.
- **Systematic Literature Organization:** Organize literature around identified themes using RDiscovery's tools, ensuring comprehensive coverage of each theme. Create connections between overlapping themes and build a structured framework for your review.
- **Synthesis and Analysis:** Leverage synthesis tools to identify patterns, consensus, and disagreements within themes. Highlight research gaps where further investigation is needed to inform your thesis contribution.

Best Practices for Effective Use

To maximize RDiscovery's impact, start with broad topic modeling to gain a holistic view of your field, then refine searches using smart filters to focus on high-impact papers. Organize literature thematically in a research log, documenting key themes, influential studies, and gaps to guide your review's structure. Use synthesis tools to draft evidence-based arguments, ensuring clarity by cross-referencing with original sources. For interdisciplinary projects, prioritize cross-disciplinary insights to enrich your review with diverse perspectives. Regularly update your search parameters to capture new publications, keeping your review current. Integrate RDiscovery with reference managers like Zotero to streamline citation organization, and export thematic summaries to your thesis document for seamless incorporation into Literature Review.

- **Quality Assurance:** Use evaluation tools to assess the quality and relevance of literature, ensuring your review reflects the field's current state. Cross-check findings with platforms like Semantic Scholar or Connected Papers for validation.

Advanced Techniques

- **Multi-Thematic Analysis:** Create multiple thematic collections to explore different aspects of your research area, ensuring comprehensive coverage and avoiding bias toward a single perspective.
- **Cross-Disciplinary Synthesis:** Use RDiscovery's ability to bridge disciplines to integrate methodologies or theories from adjacent fields, fostering innovative approaches in your review.
- **Collaborative Review Building:** Share thematic maps or synthesized insights with advisors or peers via RDiscovery's collaboration features to refine your review collaboratively.
- **Dynamic Updates:** Set up alerts for new papers within key themes to maintain an up-to-date literature review throughout your thesis process.

By harnessing RDiscovery's AI-driven navigation and synthesis capabilities, you can craft a literature review that is comprehensive, well-organized, and strategically focused. Start using RDiscovery today to map your research domain, uncover critical insights, and build a robust foundation for your thesis that sets the stage for impactful scholarship.

2.3 Consensus AI: Scientific Evidence Synthesis and Research Consensus

Consensus AI, accessible at consensus.app, is a cutting-edge academic search engine that revolutionizes the literature review process for graduate students in MS, MBA, M.Tech, M.Phil, LLM, Ph.D., D.Sc., and D.Litt. programs. Harnessing advanced language models and a database of over 220 million peer-reviewed papers, Consensus delivers evidence-based answers by extracting and synthesizing findings directly from scientific literature. Unlike traditional tools like PubMed or Google Scholar, which often return overwhelming lists of papers, Consensus uses AI to provide concise, reliable insights, highlighting areas of scientific agreement, disagreement, and gaps. This makes it an indispensable tool for Literature Review of the thesis process, where building a robust, evidence-based literature review is critical. By streamlining evidence extraction and claim verification, Consensus empowers students to construct compelling arguments, validate hypotheses, and identify research opportunities efficiently.

The platform's strength lies in its ability to interpret complex research questions and deliver synthesized results grounded in peer-reviewed studies, ensuring academic credibility. Features like the Consensus Meter visually depict the degree of scientific consensus, while advanced filters and study snapshots enable precise analysis of research quality and relevance. With a freemium model offering robust free access and premium features for enhanced functionality, Consensus is tailored for students, researchers, and professionals seeking to navigate vast academic landscapes with speed and precision. By integrating Consensus into your workflow, you can transform the literature review into a dynamic, evidence-driven process that strengthens your thesis foundation.

Core Features and Applications: Consensus AI offers a suite of features optimized for literature reviews:

- **Evidence Extraction:** Automatically extracts key findings, methodologies, and conclusions from papers, saving hours of manual reading.
- **Consensus Finding:** The Consensus Meter provides a visual snapshot of scientific agreement or disagreement across studies, helping identify robust or controversial findings.
- **Claim Verification:** Validates research claims by cross-referencing them with peer-reviewed evidence, ensuring arguments are grounded in credible sources.
- **Study Analysis:** Assesses study quality, methodology, and potential bias using quality indicators like journal prestige and study design, guiding selection of high-impact papers.
- **Confidence Scoring:** Assigns reliability scores to findings, enabling researchers to prioritize trustworthy evidence.
- **Evidence Synthesis:** Synthesizes insights across multiple studies, highlighting consensus, contradictions, and gaps to inform theoretical frameworks.
- **Knowledge Gap Identification:** Pinpoints areas of limited research or conflicting findings, guiding students toward novel thesis contributions.

Implementation Strategy: To integrate Consensus AI into your literature review:

- **Ask Precise Questions:** Input specific research questions or hypotheses (e.g., "Does mindfulness reduce workplace stress?") to leverage Consensus's natural language processing for targeted results.

- **Search and Filter Papers:** Use AI-driven search and advanced filters (e.g., study design, sample size, journal quality) to identify relevant, high-quality studies.
- **Extract and Analyze Evidence:** Review study snapshots and extracted findings to assess key insights, methodologies, and quality indicators.
- **Synthesize and Identify Consensus:** Use the Consensus Meter and synthesis tools to summarize areas of agreement, disagreement, or gaps, structuring your review around these insights.
- **Organize and Cite:** Export results to reference managers like Zotero, ensuring accurate citations and a structured bibliography.

Best Practices for Effective Use: Maximize Consensus AI's potential by crafting precise, question-driven queries to ensure focused results. Use the Consensus Meter to quickly gauge the strength of evidence, but always verify key findings by reviewing abstracts or full texts. Organize extracted insights thematically in a research log, noting consensus, controversies, and gaps to guide your review's narrative. Leverage advanced filters to prioritize recent, high-impact studies, especially for fast-evolving fields. For interdisciplinary research, explore cross-disciplinary insights to enrich your review with diverse perspectives. Regularly use the free tier's 20 monthly AI credits strategically for synthesis or Copilot features, reserving premium features for complex queries or large-scale reviews. Integrate results with tools like Avidnote for note organization to streamline your workflow.

Advanced Techniques

Multi-Question Analysis: Pose a series of related questions (e.g., broad to specific) to build a comprehensive understanding of your topic and uncover nuanced gaps.
API Integration: For advanced users, leverage Consensus's API to automate searches or integrate with custom workflows for systematic reviews.
Collaborative Synthesis: Share synthesized outputs with advisors or peers to refine arguments collaboratively, using Consensus's evidence-based insights as a foundation.
Dynamic Monitoring: Set up alerts for new papers on your topic to keep your review current throughout the thesis process.

Why Use Consensus AI?

Consensus AI is perfect for building evidence-based theoretical frameworks, supporting research arguments with credible data, and identifying controversies or gaps that shape novel research questions. Its time-efficient synthesis and precise results reduce the burden of manual literature reviews, while its focus on peer-reviewed sources ensures academic rigor. The freemium model makes it accessible, with free access to basic search and limited AI features, and premium plans unlocking unlimited synthesis and advanced tools like Pro Analysis for content drafting. By

Pro Tip

Craft specific, question-driven queries (e.g., "What is the impact of climate change on agricultural yields in developing countries?") rather than broad topics to maximize the precision of Consensus's results. Use the Consensus Meter to quickly assess the strength of evidence, and integrate findings into your thesis to build compelling, evidence-based arguments that impress advisors and committees.

using Consensus, you can craft a literature review that is not only comprehensive but also strategically aligned with your thesis goals, positioning your work for maximum impact,

By adopting Consensus AI, you can streamline your literature review, uncover critical insights, and build a robust, evidence-driven foundation for your thesis. Start today at consensus.app to transform your research process and elevate your scholarship.

2.4 Paperpal: AI-Powered Academic Writing Assistant

Paperpal, accessible at paperpal.com, is a transformative AI-powered writing assistant designed specifically for academic writing. This makes it an indispensable tool for graduate students in MS, MBA, M.Tech, M.Phil, LLM, Ph.D., D.Sc., and D.Litt. programs. Trained on millions of published scholarly articles and backed by over 23 years of expertise in scientific, technical, and medical editing, Paperpal offers a comprehensive suite of features to streamline the literature review process and enhance the quality of thesis drafts.

Unlike general-purpose tools like Grammarly or ChatGPT, Paperpal is tailored for scholarly writing, providing context-sensitive suggestions that preserve academic tone, technical terminology, and citation integrity. Its seamless integration with Microsoft Word, Google Docs, and web platforms ensures a fluid workflow, making it a powerhouse for crafting polished, publication-ready literature reviews in Chapter 2 and beyond.

The platform's strength lies in its ability to accelerate the writing process while maintaining academic rigor, addressing common challenges like language barriers, writer's block, and citation management. Paperpal's AI delivers real-time grammar, style, and clarity enhancements, alongside advanced features like reference finding, plagiarism checks, and submission readiness assessments. With a freemium model offering up to 500 free suggestions monthly and premium plans starting at $19/month, Paperpal is accessible to students while providing premium tools for complex projects. Trusted by over 1 million researchers across 125 countries and endorsed by publishers like Wolters Kluwer and IEEE, Paperpal empowers students to produce error-free, high-quality literature reviews that strengthen their thesis arguments and elevate their scholarly impact.

Why Paperpal Stands Out: Paperpal is uniquely suited for thesis writing due to its academic focus and comprehensive toolkit:

- **Scholarly Precision:** Trained on millions of peer-reviewed papers, it understands academic conventions, preserving equations, references, and field-specific jargon while offering precise language corrections.
- **Time Efficiency:** Automates tedious tasks like grammar checks, citation formatting, and literature searches, enabling students to focus on critical analysis and synthesis.
- **Global Accessibility:** Supports non-native English speakers with translation from 30+ languages and context-sensitive paraphrasing, ensuring clear, professional writing.
- **End-to-End Support:** Covers the entire writing process, from drafting and polishing to submission readiness, with tools like plagiarism detection and journal-specific checks.
- **Trusted by Experts:** Endorsed by leading publishers and used by researchers worldwide, Paperpal ensures credibility and alignment with academic standards.

Core Features and Applications: Paperpal's features are tailored to enhance every aspect of the literature review process:

- **Grammar and Style Enhancement:** Provides real-time, context-sensitive corrections for grammar, punctuation, and style, offering three times the corrections of other AI tools while retaining technical terms and references.
- **Language Polishing:** Improves clarity, readability, and flow with paraphrasing, text reduction, and academic tone adjustments, ideal for non-native speakers and complex drafts.
- **Citation and Reference Management:** Supports 10,000+ citation styles (APA, MLA, Chicago, etc.) and includes a reference finder to validate sources from 250 million+ articles, streamlining bibliography creation.
- **AI-Driven Suggestions:** Offers predictive text, outlines, abstracts, and summaries via generative AI, helping overcome writer's block and structure literature reviews effectively.
- **Research and Synthesis Tools:** Extracts key insights from papers, summarizes PDFs, and provides science-backed answers, enabling robust evidence synthesis for theoretical frameworks.
- **Plagiarism and Submission Checks:** Detects unintentional plagiarism and runs 30+ checks for journal submission readiness, ensuring compliance with academic standards.
- **Multi-Platform Integration:** Seamlessly integrates with Microsoft Word, Google Docs, and web platforms, with export options in PDF, Word, and Markdown for flexible workflows.

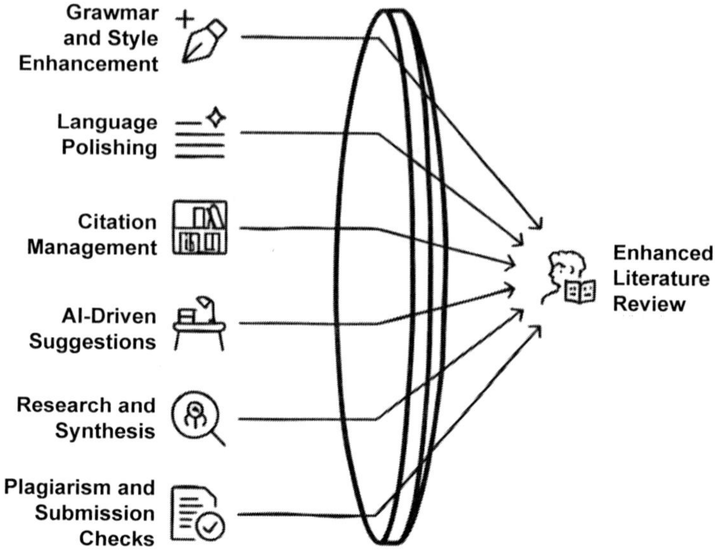

Paperpal's Comprehensive Features

Implementation Workflow: To leverage Paperpal for your literature review:

Step 1: Upload or Draft: Paste your draft or upload a document (PDF, Word) into Paperpal's web interface or use the Microsoft Word/Google Docs add-in.

Step 2: AI Analysis: Paperpal analyzes your text for grammar, style, clarity, and consistency, flagging errors and suggesting improvements tailored to academic writing.

Step 3: Apply Suggestions: Review real-time suggestions for language, tone, or structure, accepting or modifying them to suit your voice and context.

Step 4: Enhance with Research Tools: Use the Research feature to find verified sources, summarize papers, or extract insights, integrating them into your review.

Step 5: Validate and Export: Run plagiarism and submission checks, format citations, and export your polished review for inclusion in your thesis or journal submission.

Best Practices for Optimal Results: To maximize Paperpal's impact, draft your literature review in sections, using Paperpal after each to refine language and structure. Craft specific prompts for generative AI features (e.g., "Generate a literature review outline on AI in healthcare") to ensure tailored outputs. Review suggestions critically, as AI may occasionally misinterpret field-specific nuances, and cross-check references with primary sources for accuracy. Use the translation feature for non-English papers to broaden your review's scope, especially for interdisciplinary research. Save free credits for high-priority tasks like plagiarism checks, and consider the premium plan ($19/month) for unlimited suggestions and advanced features like Pro Analysis for large-scale reviews. Integrate Paperpal with tools like Zotero for citation management to create a seamless workflow.

Advanced Techniques

- **Iterative Drafting:** Use Paperpal's generative AI to create multiple outlines or summaries, refining them iteratively to align with your research objectives.
- **Cross-Disciplinary Synthesis:** Leverage the Research feature to pull insights from adjacent fields, enriching your literature review with diverse perspectives.
- **Collaborative Editing:** Share drafts with peers or advisors via Paperpal's web platform, using real-time suggestions to refine collaboratively.
- **Submission Optimization:** Run journal-specific submission checks to tailor your review to target publications, increasing acceptance chances.

Pro Tip

Use Paperpal after drafting each thesis chapter to polish language and ensure academic tone, but always review AI suggestions to maintain your unique voice. For literature reviews, combine Paperpal's Research feature with Connected Papers or Consensus AI to validate sources and synthesize findings, creating a robust, evidence-based narrative that impresses examiners.

Researchers praise Paperpal for its academic focus, with one noting, "It doesn't make mistakes like Grammarly and has perfectly edited every essay," while another highlighted its ability to save time on literature searches and drafting. However, some users report occasional performance issues or clunky citation management, suggesting manual review of citations. Despite these, Paperpal's precision and integration make it a top choice for thesis writing.

By adopting Paperpal, you can transform your literature review into a polished, evidence-driven masterpiece. Start today at paperpal.com to streamline your writing, enhance clarity, and deliver a thesis that stands out for its scholarly excellence.

2.5 Enago Read: AI-Powered Academic Reading Assistant

Enago Read, accessible at read.enago.com, is a cutting-edge AI-powered reading assistant designed to revolutionize the literature review process for graduate students in MS, MBA, M.Tech, M.Phil, LLM, Ph.D., D.Sc., and D.Litt. programs. Formerly known as RAx, this platform, developed by Crimson Interactive, leverages proprietary AI models trained on over 200 million scholarly articles to streamline the exploration, comprehension, and organization of academic literature. Unlike traditional PDF readers or generic AI tools, Enago Read is tailored for academic research, offering features like smart PDF analysis, auto-summarization, multi-language translation, and collaborative workspaces that accelerate the review process while enhancing understanding of complex texts. Its intuitive interface and robust functionality make it an essential tool for Chapter 2, where synthesizing vast amounts of literature into a coherent narrative is critical.

The platform's strength lies in its ability to process and organize large volumes of research papers efficiently, reducing the time spent on manual reading and note-taking. Enago Read's AI-driven features, such as key insight extraction, contextual recommendations, and customizable critique templates, enable students to grasp core findings, identify research gaps, and structure their reviews with precision. With a freemium model offering a free trial and premium plans starting at $3/month, it provides accessible, high-value tools for researchers worldwide. Endorsed by users like Ph.D. students at IIT Gandhinagar and DA-IICT for its distraction-free reading and organizational capabilities, Enago Read empowers students to build comprehensive, evidence-based literature reviews that elevate their thesis quality.

Why Enago Read Excels: Enago Read stands out as a premier tool for literature reviews due to its academic-specific design and comprehensive functionality:

- **Rapid Comprehension:** Processes papers up to three times faster than manual reading with AI-generated summaries and key insights, ideal for managing large literature sets.
- **Contextual Understanding:** The Copilot feature allows real-time questioning of papers, clarifying complex concepts and methodologies for deeper comprehension.

- **Global Accessibility:** Supports translation in over 30 languages, enabling non-native English speakers to engage with diverse literature effortlessly.
- **Collaborative Efficiency:** Facilitates teamwork through shared workspaces, allowing students to collaborate with advisors or peers on literature analysis.
- **Secure and Scalable:** Built with end-to-end encryption and proprietary data pipelines, it ensures data privacy while handling thousands of articles daily.

Core Features and Applications: Enago Read's features are optimized for efficient literature review workflows:

- **Smart PDF Analysis and Navigation:** Imports and analyzes PDFs, extracting structure, figures, and references for seamless navigation and comprehension.
- **Auto-Summarization:** Generates concise summaries of key sections, abstracts, and findings, enabling quick relevance assessments and reducing information overload.
- **Multi-Language Translation:** Translates papers in over 30 languages, broadening access to global research and supporting interdisciplinary reviews.
- **Smart Notes and Annotations:** AI-generated annotations and customizable critique templates help organize insights, track gaps, and structure arguments.
- **Intelligent Highlighting and Bookmarking:** Highlights key text and bookmarks critical sections, with split-view comparisons to streamline critical analysis.
- **Literature Discovery:** Recommends related papers, theses, and resources from institutional libraries, uncovering hidden sources for comprehensive reviews.
- **Collaboration and Export:** Supports shared reading lists and integrates with Zotero and Mendeley for citation management and export in multiple formats.

Implementation Workflow: To leverage Enago Read for your literature review:

- **Step 1: Upload Documents:** Import PDFs or documents via the web platform or browser extension, supporting seamless integration with existing libraries.
- **Step 2: Generate Summaries:** Use auto-summarization to extract abstracts, key findings, and methodologies, prioritizing relevant papers for review.
- **Step 3: Annotate and Organize:** Create smart notes and annotations using AI suggestions, organizing insights into customizable critique templates for thematic analysis.
- **Step 4: Explore and Collaborate:** Use the Copilot feature to ask questions about papers, share reading lists with peers, and discover related literature for broader context.
- **Step 5: Export and Integrate:** Export summaries, notes, and citations to reference managers or thesis drafts, ensuring a cohesive workflow.

Best Practices for Optimal Results: Start with Enago Read's AI summaries to quickly assess paper relevance, then dive into specific sections for deeper analysis. Use the Copilot feature to clarify complex methodologies or terms, especially for interdisciplinary or technical papers. Organize notes thematically using critique templates, documenting gaps and connections to guide your review's structure. Leverage translation for non-English papers to expand your literature scope, and use the discovery feature to uncover hidden sources from institutional libraries. Regularly share annotated papers with advisors via collaborative workspaces to refine your analysis. Integrate with Zotero for citation management, and export summaries to your thesis document for seamless incorporation into Chapter 2. Use the free trial to test core features, reserving premium plans for large-scale reviews or collaborative projects.

Pro Tip

Begin with Enago Read's AI summaries to prioritize relevant papers, then use the Copilot feature to ask targeted questions (e.g., "What are the main methodologies in this paper?") for deeper understanding. Organize insights with critique templates and share them with advisors to refine your literature review, ensuring a robust, evidence-based narrative for your thesis.

By adopting Enago Read, you can process papers faster, understand complex texts with ease, and organize insights into a compelling literature review. Start today at read.enago.com to streamline your research workflow and elevate your thesis to new heights of scholarly excellence.

In Conclusion, Chapter 2 has unveiled the transformative power of AI tools in redefining the literature review process for graduate students. Navigating the overwhelming expanse of academic literature—over 3 million new papers annually as of June 2025—demands efficiency and precision. Tools like Connected Papers, RDiscovery, Consensus AI, Enago Read, and Paperpal empower researchers to streamline discovery, analysis, and synthesis, turning a daunting task into a strategic advantage. Each tool targets a specific aspect of the literature review, from mapping research networks to polishing scholarly prose, enabling students to craft comprehensive, evidence-based reviews that strengthen their thesis foundation. Paperpal, in particular, shines as an all-in-one writing assistant, ensuring clarity, academic rigor, and citation accuracy across all chapters.

- **Connected Papers:** This tool revolutionizes literature exploration with dynamic citation network visualizations, revealing intellectual connections and research clusters. Ideal for mapping the historical and thematic evolution of a field, it helps students identify influential papers, interdisciplinary links, and research gaps through its "Prior Works" and "Derivative Works" features. Use Connected Papers early in Chapter 2 to build a visual overview of your research landscape and uncover novel opportunities for your thesis.

- **RDiscovery:** RDiscovery excels in organizing complex literature into guided thematic pathways, using AI-driven topic modeling to highlight key themes and relationships. Its synthesis tools identify consensus, contradictions, and gaps, making it perfect for structuring a coherent review. Leverage RDiscovery to systematically organize literature and align your research with emerging trends, ensuring a comprehensive and focused Chapter 2 narrative.
- **Consensus AI:** Designed for evidence synthesis, Consensus AI extracts key findings from over 220 million papers, providing a Consensus Meter to visualize scientific agreement or disagreement. Its claim verification and study quality analysis ensure credible, evidence-based arguments. Use Consensus AI to validate hypotheses, identify controversies, and build robust theoretical frameworks, making it a cornerstone for evidence-driven literature reviews.
- **Enago Read:** Enago Read accelerates comprehension of large literature volumes with AI-powered PDF analysis, auto-summarization, and multi-language translation. Its smart annotations and collaborative workspaces streamline note-taking and insight organization. Start with Enago Read to process papers three times faster, organize insights thematically, and broaden your review with global, interdisciplinary sources.
- **Paperpal:** The standout tool for academic writing, Paperpal transforms drafts into polished, publication-

ready reviews with context-sensitive grammar, style, and citation support. Trained on millions of scholarly articles, it offers real-time suggestions, reference finding, and plagiarism checks, saving hours of editing time. Integrate Paperpal across all chapters, especially Chapter 2, to ensure clarity, maintain scholarly tone, and produce a professional narrative that impresses examiners.

To maximize these tools, combine their strengths: use Connected Papers for exploration, RDiscovery for organization, Consensus AI for synthesis, Enago Read for rapid reading, and Paperpal for polishing. Start today by selecting one tool—Paperpal for immediate draft refinement or Consensus AI for evidence validation—and build a tailored workflow. Document AI usage transparently to uphold ethical standards, and consult advisors to refine insights. These tools empower you to craft a literature review that is not only comprehensive but also a powerful springboard for your thesis's originality and impact. Act now—leverage these AI tools to streamline Chapter 2 and elevate your scholarship to new heights.

Chapter 3

Methodology and Research Design

Crafting a robust methodology section is a cornerstone of thesis development for graduate students pursuing MS, MBA, M.Tech, M.Phil, LLM, Ph.D., D.Sc., and D.Litt. degrees, as it establishes the credibility and rigor of your research. This critical component requires a clear articulation of research methods, data collection strategies, and analytical frameworks, ensuring alignment with your research questions and objectives. Traditionally, developing a methodology involves labor-intensive tasks: scouring methodological literature, evaluating study designs, and structuring workflows that balance feasibility with academic standards. With over 3 million scholarly articles published annually as of June 2025, navigating this landscape to design an innovative yet practical methodology can be overwhelming, particularly for interdisciplinary or novel research.

AI-powered tools have revolutionized this process by automating literature analysis, suggesting tailored methodological frameworks, and streamlining research design workflows. Platforms like Thesis AI, Scholarcy, Notebook LLM, SciSummary, and Manus AI empower students to craft methodologies that are precise, evidence-based, and aligned with their research goals. These tools handle repetitive tasks—such as summarizing methodological papers, identifying relevant study designs, or generating analytical templates—freeing researchers to focus on critical decision-making and theoretical integration.

By leveraging AI, students can enhance the rigor, coherence, and originality of their methodology section, ensuring it withstands academic scrutiny and supports impactful scholarship.

The key to a strong methodology lies in combining AI-driven insights with human expertise. AI excels at processing vast datasets, detecting methodological trends, and proposing structured designs, but researchers must validate outputs, ensure ethical compliance, and contextualize methods within their study's framework. Tools like Thesis AI guide hypothesis-driven design, Scholarcy extracts methodological insights, Notebook LLM organizes research protocols, SciSummary condenses complex studies, and Manus AI refines analytical approaches. Together, they enable students to design methodologies that are both innovative and robust. Embrace these tools to streamline your methodology development, avoid common pitfalls, and build a research foundation that elevates your thesis. Start integrating these AI solutions today to craft a methodology section that sets your work apart.

3.1 Scholarcy: AI Research Summarization and Analysis

Scholarcy, accessible at scholarcy.com, is an AI-powered research assistant that revolutionizes the methodology development process for graduate students in MS, MBA, M.Tech, M.Phil, LLM, Ph.D., D.Sc., and D.Litt. programs. Designed to streamline the analysis of academic literature, Scholarcy transforms complex research papers, book chapters, and reports into concise, structured summaries and interactive flashcards, enabling rapid comprehension and organization of methodological insights. Unlike traditional methods that require hours of manual reading and note-taking, Scholarcy's proprietary algorithms extract key findings, methodologies, and references with precision, making it an essential tool for crafting the methodology section of a thesis. Its ability to break down dense texts into digestible formats, coupled with seamless integration with tools like Zotero and Mendeley, empowers students to design rigorous, evidence-based research methodologies efficiently.

The platform's strength lies in its focus on simplifying the analysis of methodological literature, enabling students to identify relevant study designs, data collection strategies, and analytical frameworks in minutes. With features like smart highlighting, customizable summaries, and literature matrix generation, Scholarcy supports the development of a coherent methodology by highlighting gaps, comparing approaches, and organizing insights. Its freemium model offers up to three daily summaries for free, with premium plans starting at $9.99/month or $90/year, unlocking unlimited summarization and advanced features like flashcard exports. Trusted by over 1 million users, including students with ADHD or dyslexia for its accessibility features, Scholarcy is a game-changer for crafting a methodology section that is both robust and time-efficient.

Scholarcy outperforms traditional methods in several ways:

- **Speed and Efficiency:** Reduces the time to analyze methodological papers from hours to minutes by generating structured summaries and extracting key study designs, compared to manual skimming and note-taking.
- **Precision Extraction:** Identifies methodologies, participant details, and limitations with high accuracy, ensuring students focus on relevant, high-quality studies.
- **Accessibility for All:** Supports neurodivergent students with text-to-speech, adjustable text sizes, and structured flashcards, making complex texts more approachable.

- **Integration and Organization:** Seamlessly integrates with reference managers and exports summaries to Excel or Word, streamlining methodology organization.
- **Scalability:** Handles multiple document types (PDFs, Word, URLs) and large literature sets, ideal for comprehensive methodological reviews.

Scholarcy's features are tailored to support methodology development:

- **Smart Summarization:** Converts papers into interactive summary flashcards, extracting methodologies, findings, and limitations, enabling quick assessment of study designs.
- **Robo-Highlighter:** Automatically highlights key methodological sections (e.g., study design, data collection, analysis) for focused analysis.
- **Reference Extraction:** Pulls citations and links to open-access versions, simplifying validation and integration into your methodology.
- **Literature Matrix Generation:** Creates comparative tables of methods, participants, and outcomes across papers, aiding in methodological synthesis.
- **Customizable Summaries:** Adjusts summary depth (from one-sentence overviews to detailed breakdowns) to match research needs.
- **Cross-Format Compatibility:** Processes PDFs, Word documents, URLs, and videos, with browser extensions for Chrome and Edge to summarize web content.
- **Personal Library:** Organizes summaries and flashcards in a searchable library, exportable to Zotero, Mendeley, or Excel for seamless workflow integration.

Comparison to Traditional Methods: Traditional methodology development involves manually reading dozens of papers, extracting relevant methods, and organizing notes—a process that can take weeks and risks missing critical insights due to human error or bias. Scholarcy accelerates this by:

- **Reducing Time:** Summarizes papers in 5–10 minutes versus 15–60 minutes per paper manually, enabling students to review more studies in less time.
- **Enhancing Accuracy:** Uses AI trained on millions of papers to extract methodologies with precision, minimizing oversight compared to manual skimming.
- **Improving Organization:** Generates structured flashcards and matrices, replacing scattered notes with a cohesive framework for methodology design.
- **Supporting Synthesis:** Compares methods across papers, highlighting trends and gaps that inform innovative study designs, unlike linear note-taking.
- **Accessibility:** Offers tools like text-to-speech and flashcards, making methodological literature more accessible than traditional reading, especially for neurodivergent students.

Strong Methodology Section with Scholarcy

Step 1: Import Documents: Upload PDFs, Word files, or URLs of methodological papers via Scholarcy's web platform or browser extension.
Step 2: Generate Summaries: Use smart summarization to extract study designs, data collection methods, and analytical approaches, customizing summary depth as needed.
Step 3: Analyze Methodologies: Review highlighted sections and flashcards to identify relevant methods, focusing on study design and limitations.
Step 4: Build a Literature Matrix: Export comparative tables to Excel to synthesize methodologies across papers, identifying trends and gaps.
Step 5: Integrate and Validate: Export summaries and references to Zotero or Mendeley, cross-checking primary sources to ensure accuracy and alignment with your research objectives.

Best Practices for Student Adoption: To effectively adopt Scholarcy for your methodology section:

- **Start Early:** Begin using Scholarcy to summarize methodological papers as soon as you define your research questions, ensuring a broad foundation.
- **Customize Summaries:** Adjust summary settings (e.g., "Researcher" for detailed methods) to focus on study designs relevant to your thesis.
- **Organize Systematically:** Use the personal library to categorize summaries by methodology type (e.g., qualitative, quantitative) and export matrices to structure your review.
- **Validate Outputs:** Cross-check AI-generated summaries with original papers to ensure accuracy, especially for niche or complex methodologies.
- **Leverage Free Tier:** Use the free plan's three daily summaries for initial exploration, upgrading to premium for large-scale reviews or flashcard exports.
- **Integrate with Workflow:** Pair Scholarcy with tools like Zotero for citation management or Paperpal for draft polishing to create a seamless methodology workflow.
- **Support Accessibility:** Utilize text-to-speech and flashcard features to enhance comprehension, particularly for neurodivergent students or non-native speakers.

Advanced Techniques

- **Methodological Comparison:** Use literature matrices to compare study designs across disciplines, identifying innovative approaches for interdisciplinary theses.
- **Gap Identification:** Analyze flashcards for under-explored methods or limitations, guiding the development of novel research designs.

- **Collaborative Review:** Share summaries with advisors or peers via exported flashcards to refine methodological choices collaboratively.
- **Dynamic Updates:** Revisit your library to incorporate new papers, ensuring your methodology remains current with emerging research trends.

> **Pro Tip**
>
> Start with Scholarcy's summary flashcards to quickly identify relevant methodologies, then use the literature matrix feature to compare study designs and pinpoint gaps. Combine with Paperpal for polishing your methodology section to ensure a clear, rigorous, and professional narrative that impresses examiners.

By adopting Scholarcy, students can craft a methodology section that is faster, more precise, and better organized than traditional methods. Start today at scholarcy.com to streamline your research process, enhance methodological rigor, and build a thesis that stands out for its scholarly excellence.

3.2 NotebookLM: AI-Driven Research Organization and Workflow Design

NotebookLM, developed by Google and accessible via notebooklm.google.com, is an innovative AI-powered research tool that transforms the methodology development process for graduate students in MS, MBA, M.Tech, M.Phil, LLM, Ph.D., D.Sc., and D.Litt. programs. Designed as a virtual research assistant, NotebookLM leverages Google's advanced Gemini 1.5 AI model to organize, analyze, and synthesize research materials, enabling students to craft robust, well-structured methodology sections with efficiency and precision.

Unlike traditional methods that rely on scattered notes and manual organization, NotebookLM creates a centralized, interactive workspace where students can upload up to 50 sources (PDFs, web pages, or text), generate summaries, pose questions, and design methodological workflows. Its ability to produce tailored outputs like study guides, timelines, and FAQs makes it an essential tool for developing a coherent and rigorous methodology section in a thesis.

The platform's strength lies in its conversational AI, which allows students to interact with their sources as if consulting a research partner, extracting methodological insights, identifying study designs, and organizing complex workflows. With features like audio overviews, collaborative sharing, and exportable outputs, NotebookLM streamlines the process of aligning research questions with appropriate methods, ensuring feasibility and academic rigor. Available for free with a Google account, it supports up to 25 notebooks with 50 sources each, making it accessible and scalable for students. By integrating NotebookLM, researchers can save hours of manual work, avoid methodological missteps, and craft a methodology section that is both innovative and aligned with their thesis objectives.

NotebookLM outperforms traditional methods by offering:

- **Centralized Organization:** Consolidates up to 50 sources per notebook, replacing scattered notes with a searchable, AI-organized workspace.
- **Conversational Analysis:** Allows students to ask specific questions about methodologies (e.g., "What data collection methods are used in these studies?"), delivering tailored insights instantly.
- **Workflow Efficiency:** Generates timelines, outlines, and study guides to structure research designs, streamlining methodology planning.

- **Collaborative Flexibility:** Enables sharing with advisors or peers for real-time feedback, enhancing methodological rigor.
- **Accessibility:** Free access with no subscription required, ideal for students with budget constraints.

NotebookLM's features are tailored to support methodology development:

- **Source Analysis and Summarization:** Uploads PDFs, web pages, or text (up to 200,000 words per source) and generates concise summaries of methodologies, study designs, and limitations, highlighting relevant insights.
- **Conversational Querying:** Uses Gemini 1.5 to answer specific questions about research methods, data collection, or analytical frameworks, enabling targeted exploration of methodological literature.
- **Workflow Design Tools:** Creates timelines, outlines, and FAQs to structure research protocols, aligning methods with research questions and objectives.
- **Interactive Notebooks:** Organizes sources, notes, and AI-generated content in a centralized workspace, with pinning and tagging for easy retrieval.
- **Audio Overviews:** Produces podcast-style summaries of methodological insights, ideal for auditory learners or reviewing complex studies on the go.
- **Collaborative Sharing:** Shares notebooks with advisors or peers for collaborative refinement, with secure Google Drive integration.
- **Exportable Outputs:** Generates downloadable summaries, outlines, or tables in text or Markdown, integrable with tools like Zotero or Paperpal.

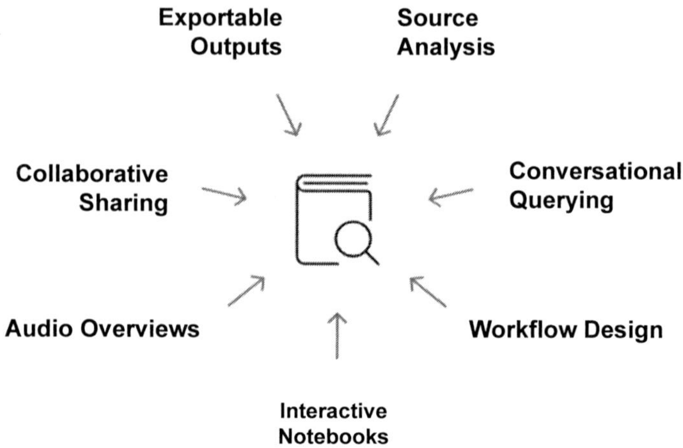

NotebookLM's Features for Methodology Development

Comparison to Traditional Methods: Traditional methodology development involves manually reviewing literature, extracting methods, and drafting workflows, often taking weeks and risking oversight due to human error. NotebookLM offers:

- **Faster Processing:** Summarizes and queries multiple sources in minutes, compared to hours per paper manually.
- **Enhanced Precision:** Extracts specific methodological details with AI accuracy, reducing the risk of missing critical insights.
- **Structured Organization:** Replaces disorganized notes with interactive notebooks and timelines, ensuring a cohesive research design.
- **Dynamic Interaction:** Allows real-time questioning of sources, unlike static note-taking, enabling deeper methodological understanding.
- **Scalability:** Handles large literature sets effortlessly, ideal for comprehensive or interdisciplinary methodology reviews.

To craft a strong methodology section with NotebookLM:

Step 1: Create a Notebook: Set up a new notebook on notebooklm.google.com and upload 5–10 methodological papers or relevant sources.

Step 2: Summarize Sources: Use AI to generate summaries of study designs, data collection methods, and analytical frameworks, focusing on relevance to your research.

Step 3: Query Methodologies: Ask specific questions (e.g., "Which studies use mixed-methods designs?") to extract tailored insights and compare approaches.

Step 4: Design Workflow: Generate timelines or outlines to structure your research protocol, aligning methods with objectives and feasibility constraints.

Step 5: Collaborate and Export: Share the notebook with advisors for feedback, then export outputs to your thesis document or reference manager.

To effectively adopt NotebookLM:

- **Start with Focused Sources:** Upload a curated set of methodological papers to ensure relevant AI outputs, avoiding overly broad sources.
- **Ask Precise Questions:** Frame queries specifically (e.g., "What are the sampling methods in these studies?") to extract actionable methodological insights.
- **Organize Systematically:** Use pinning and tagging to categorize sources by method type (e.g., qualitative, quantitative) or research stage.
- **Validate AI Outputs:** Cross-check AI-generated summaries with original papers to ensure accuracy, especially for niche methodologies.

- **Leverage Collaboration:** Share notebooks with advisors to refine your research design, incorporating their feedback for rigor.
- **Integrate with Workflow:** Pair NotebookLM with Scholarcy for summarization or Paperpal for draft polishing, creating a seamless methodology workflow.
- **Use Audio Overviews:** Listen to podcast-style summaries to review complex methods on the go, enhancing comprehension for auditory learners.

Advanced Techniques

- **Multi-Source Synthesis:** Query multiple sources simultaneously to compare methodologies across disciplines, identifying innovative approaches.
- **Iterative Design:** Generate multiple timeline or outline iterations to test different research designs, selecting the most robust for your thesis.
- **Collaborative Workshops:** Use shared notebooks to host brainstorming sessions with peers, refining methodological choices collectively.
- **Dynamic Updates:** Add new sources to your notebook as research evolves, ensuring your methodology stays current with emerging trends.

Users, including Ph.D. students, praise NotebookLM for its ability to "organize and make sense of dozens of papers in minutes" and its podcast-style overviews for accessibility (Reddit feedback). Some note limitations in handling highly technical equations, suggesting manual review for such content. Its free access and collaborative features make it a top choice for methodology development.

Pro Tip

Use NotebookLM's conversational querying to ask targeted questions about methodological details (e.g., "What statistical methods are used in these papers?"), then export timelines to structure your methodology section. Combine with Paperpal to polish your draft, ensuring a clear, rigorous narrative that aligns with your research objectives.

By adopting NotebookLM, students can craft a methodology section that is faster, more organized, and rigorously aligned with their research goals. Start today at notebooklm.google.com to streamline your research design and elevate your thesis to new heights of scholarly excellence.

3.3 Thesis AI: AI-Powered Methodological Drafting and Citation Synthesis

Thesis AI, accessible at thesisai.io, is a cutting-edge AI-powered platform designed to streamline methodology development for graduate students in MS, MBA, M.Tech, M.Phil, LLM, Ph.D., D.Sc., and D.Litt. programs. Unlike traditional tools that focus solely on literature review or writing, Thesis AI specializes in generating structured scientific documents, including methodology sections, by processing up to 100 research papers with a single prompt. Leveraging advanced large language models (LLMs), it produces LaTeX-formatted drafts with inline citations, ensuring academic rigor and seamless integration with tools like Overleaf. This makes Thesis AI an invaluable asset for crafting a precise, evidence-based methodology section, enabling students to design robust research frameworks efficiently.

The platform's strength lies in its ability to synthesize methodological insights from vast literature sets and generate tailored research designs that align with specific research questions. With features like customizable document structuring, citation style flexibility (APA, IEEE, Chicago, etc.), and page-level citation options, Thesis AI empowers students to create methodologies that are both comprehensive and adaptable. Its subscription-based model (pricing available on the website) supports high-volume document processing, making it ideal for complex theses. By automating literature synthesis and methodological drafting, Thesis AI saves hours compared to traditional methods, allowing students to focus on refining their research design and ensuring alignment with academic standards.

Thesis AI stands out for its methodological focus and efficiency:

- **Rapid Synthesis:** Processes up to 100 papers to extract methodologies, study designs, and analytical frameworks, reducing weeks of manual work to minutes.
- **Customizable Outputs:** Allows users to specify document structure (e.g., methodology sections, subsections) and citation styles, ensuring alignment with thesis requirements.
- **Citation Precision:** Supports paper- and page-level citations, enhancing traceability and credibility in methodological literature reviews.
- **LaTeX Integration:** Produces LaTeX-formatted drafts compatible with Overleaf, streamlining professional document preparation.
- **Academic Integrity:** Generates original drafts with verifiable citations, though manual review is advised to ensure compliance with institutional guidelines.

Thesis AI's features are optimized for methodology development:

- **Literature Synthesis:** Analyzes up to 100 uploaded papers to extract methodologies, data collection methods, and analytical techniques, synthesizing them into a cohesive draft.
- **Prompt-Based Drafting:** Generates methodology sections based on user prompts (e.g., "Create a mixed-methods design for studying AI adoption in education"), tailoring outputs to research objectives.
- **Citation Management:** Supports multiple citation styles (APA, MLA, Chicago, IEEE, etc.) with paper- or page-level inline citations, ensuring accurate referencing.
- **Document Structuring:** Allows customization of section headings, subsections, and content focus, aligning the methodology with thesis requirements.
- **Export to LaTeX:** Produces LaTeX files for seamless editing in Overleaf, ideal for technical or scientific theses requiring precise formatting.
- **Multi-Language Support:** Generates drafts in various languages, with manual translation options to bypass AI detection, ensuring flexibility for global researchers.
- **Error Handling:** Flags potential citation syntax issues, with fixes available via Overleaf integration, ensuring polished outputs.

Comparison to Traditional Methods: Traditional methodology development involves manually reviewing literature, extracting methods, and drafting designs, often taking weeks and risking inconsistencies due to human oversight. Thesis AI offers:

- **Time Efficiency:** Synthesizes literature and drafts methodologies in minutes, compared to days or weeks of manual work.

- **Comprehensive Analysis:** Processes large literature sets to identify diverse methodological approaches, reducing bias compared to selective manual reading.
- **Structured Outputs:** Generates organized, LaTeX-formatted drafts with inline citations, replacing scattered notes and manual formatting.
- **Scalability:** Handles complex, interdisciplinary methodologies, unlike manual methods that struggle with large or diverse datasets.
- **Precision:** Ensures accurate citation integration, minimizing errors common in manual bibliography creation.

To Craft a Strong Methodology Section with Thesis AI

Step 1: Upload Sources: Import up to 100 PDFs or text files of methodological papers via the Thesis AI platform.
Step 2: Define Prompt: Specify your research objectives and desired methodology structure (e.g., "Draft a quantitative methodology for studying renewable energy adoption").
Step 3: Generate Draft: Use Thesis AI to synthesize methods from sources and produce a LaTeX-formatted methodology section with inline citations.
Step 4: Refine and Edit: Review the draft in Thesis AI or export to Overleaf for manual adjustments, ensuring alignment with your research context.
Step 5: Validate Citations: Check citation accuracy and format, cross-referencing with original sources to maintain academic integrity.

Best Practices for Student Adoption: To effectively adopt Thesis AI:

- **Curate Relevant Sources:** Upload high-quality, relevant papers to ensure accurate methodological synthesis, avoiding overly broad or irrelevant sources.

- **Craft Specific Prompts:** Use detailed prompts (e.g., "Generate a qualitative methodology with thematic analysis for mental health studies") to tailor outputs to your thesis needs.
- **Review Outputs Critically:** Validate AI-generated methods against original papers and institutional guidelines to ensure feasibility and rigor.
- **Leverage LaTeX Integration:** Export drafts to Overleaf for professional formatting, especially for technical or STEM theses.
- **Integrate with Workflow:** Pair Thesis AI with Scholarcy for summarization or Paperpal for polishing to streamline methodology development.
- **Ensure Ethical Use:** Document AI usage transparently and manually refine outputs to reflect your intellectual contribution, avoiding AI detection issues.
- **Start Small:** Begin with a single methodology section to test Thesis AI's capabilities, scaling to larger drafts as needed.

Advanced Techniques

- **Interdisciplinary Synthesis:** Upload papers from multiple disciplines to generate hybrid methodologies, fostering innovative research designs.
- **Iterative Drafting:** Generate multiple drafts with varied prompts to explore different methodological approaches, selecting the most robust.
- **Citation Optimization:** Use page-level citations for detailed literature reviews, enhancing traceability in complex methodologies.
- **Collaborative Refinement:** Share LaTeX drafts with advisors via Overleaf for feedback, ensuring methodological alignment.

Pro Tip

Craft precise prompts to generate tailored methodology drafts (e.g., "Design a mixed-methods study with survey and interview protocols for educational research"), then refine in Overleaf and polish with Paperpal to ensure a rigorous, professional methodology section that aligns with your thesis goals.

Users highlight Thesis AI's ability to "process dozens of papers into a structured methodology in minutes," though some note occasional BibTeX syntax errors, easily fixed in Overleaf. Its focus on LaTeX and citation synthesis makes it ideal for STEM and technical theses, but manual validation is recommended to ensure academic integrity.

By adopting Thesis AI, students can craft a methodology section that is faster, more comprehensive, and rigorously cited than traditional methods. Start today at thesisai.io to streamline your research design and elevate your thesis to new heights of scholarly excellence.

3.4 SciSummary: AI-Powered Scientific Article Summarization

SciSummary, accessible at scisummary.com, is an AI-driven summarization tool designed to accelerate methodology development for graduate students in MS, MBA, M.Tech, M.Phil, LLM, Ph.D., D.Sc., and D.Litt. programs. Powered by advanced AI models like GPT-3.5 and GPT-4, and guided by a team of PhDs, SciSummary transforms complex scientific articles into concise, accurate summaries, extracting key methodologies, findings, and limitations.

Unlike traditional methods that require hours of manual reading to identify relevant study designs, SciSummary processes papers up to 200,000 words in minutes, supporting PDFs, DOCX, TXT, and web links. With over 1.5 million papers summarized for 700,000+ users since March 2023, including researchers at major U.S. universities, SciSummary is a trusted tool for crafting robust methodology sections.

The platform's strength lies in its ability to handle large literature sets, analyze figures and tables, and provide customizable summaries, making it ideal for synthesizing methodological insights. Features like semantic search, multi-document comparison, and chat functionality enable students to explore study designs, compare methods, and identify gaps efficiently. Its freemium model offers 10,000 words monthly for free, with paid plans starting at $4.99/month for 1 million words. SciSummary's user-friendly dashboard and Zotero integration streamline methodology development, ensuring students can design rigorous, evidence-based research frameworks faster than traditional approaches.

SciSummary outperforms traditional methods by:

- **Speed:** Summarizes papers in minutes, compared to hours of manual reading per article, enabling rapid methodological analysis.
- **Bulk Processing:** Handles multiple papers simultaneously, ideal for comprehensive methodology reviews across large datasets.
- **Data Analysis:** Extracts insights from figures and tables, enhancing understanding of complex methodological designs.
- **Accessibility:** Offers a free tier and affordable plans, with a user-friendly interface for all researchers.

- **Academic Focus:** Preserves technical accuracy while simplifying jargon, ensuring relevance for thesis methodology sections.

SciSummary's features are tailored for methodology development:

- **Advanced Summarization:** Generates concise summaries of methodologies, study designs, and data collection techniques using GPT-3.5 and GPT-4, guided by PhD expertise.
- **Multi-Document Analysis:** Combines summaries of multiple papers to provide an overview of methodological trends, ideal for comparative analysis.
- **Semantic Search:** Identifies papers addressing specific methods or questions (e.g., "What statistical methods are used?"), streamlining methodological exploration.
- **Figure and Table Analysis:** Extracts data from visuals, clarifying complex methodological details for accurate synthesis.
- **Chat Functionality:** Allows users to ask follow-up questions about methods, enhancing understanding of study designs.
- **Reference Management:** Integrates with Zotero for seamless citation import and organization, supporting bibliography creation.
- **Customizable Outputs:** Adjusts summary length and focus (e.g., methodology-specific) to align with research needs.

Comparison to Traditional Methods: Traditional methodology development involves manually reading papers, extracting methods, and organizing notes, often taking weeks and risking oversight. SciSummary offers:

- **Time Savings:** Summarizes 25 papers in under an hour, compared to days manually, enabling faster methodology design.
- **Comprehensive Insights:** Analyzes large literature sets to identify diverse methods, reducing bias from selective reading.
- **Structured Synthesis:** Generates comparative summaries and tables, replacing scattered notes with organized frameworks.
- **Enhanced Accuracy:** Leverages AI and PhD oversight to ensure precise extraction of methodological details, minimizing errors.
- **Scalability:** Processes lengthy documents and bulk uploads, ideal for interdisciplinary or complex methodologies.

To Craft a Strong Methodology Section with SciSummary

Step 1: Upload Sources: Import PDFs, DOCX, or links via the dashboard or email, or connect Zotero for seamless access.
Step 2: Generate Summaries: Run single or bulk summaries to extract methodologies, focusing on study design and data analysis.
Step 3: Query Specifics: Use semantic search or chat to explore methods (e.g., "What qualitative methods are used?") and compare approaches.
Step 4: Synthesize Insights: Create a combined summary or comparison table to identify trends, gaps, or suitable methods.
Step 5: Export and Integrate: Export summaries to Zotero or Word, integrating into your methodology section with Paperpal for polishing.

Best Practices for Student Adoption: To effectively adopt SciSummary:

- **Curate Relevant Papers:** Upload methodology-focused papers to ensure targeted summaries, avoiding irrelevant content.
- **Use Specific Queries:** Ask precise questions via chat (e.g., "What sampling methods are used in these studies?") to extract actionable insights.
- **Leverage Free Tier:** Use the 10,000-word free plan to test summarization, reserving paid plans ($4.99/month) for bulk analysis.
- **Validate Outputs:** Cross-check summaries with original papers to ensure accuracy, especially for technical methods.
- **Integrate with Workflow:** Pair with NotebookLM for organization or Paperpal for draft refinement to streamline methodology development.
- **Organize Summaries:** Tag papers by method type (e.g., experimental, survey) in the dashboard for easy retrieval.
- **Expand Insights:** Use the "Expand" feature to dive deeper into specific methodological details, avoiding overgeneralization.

Advanced Techniques

- **Comparative Analysis:** Run "Compare" summaries to contrast methodologies across papers, identifying optimal designs for your thesis.
- **Gap Identification:** Use semantic search to find under-explored methods, guiding innovative research designs.
- **Interdisciplinary Synthesis:** Analyze papers from multiple fields to develop hybrid methodologies for complex studies.

- **Dynamic Updates:** Add new papers to your library to keep your methodology current with emerging research trends.

<u>**Pro Tip**</u>

Start with SciSummary's "Combine" summary to get an overview of methodologies across multiple papers, then use semantic search to pinpoint specific methods. Pair with Paperpal to polish your methodology draft, ensuring a rigorous, well-cited section that aligns with your thesis goals.

Users praise SciSummary for its speed and accuracy, with one noting, "It's a game-changer for summarizing complex articles in minutes". Some caution that expanding on topics not covered in the source can lead to inaccuracies, recommending careful prompt crafting. Its affordability and Zotero integration make it a favorite for students.

By adopting SciSummary, students can craft a methodology section that is faster, more comprehensive, and rigorously informed. Start today at scisummary.com to streamline your research design and elevate your thesis to new heights of scholarly excellence.

3.5 Manus AI: Autonomous Research Design and Analysis

Manus AI, accessible at manus.im, is a groundbreaking autonomous AI agent developed by Monica (formerly Butterfly Effect), a Wuhan-based startup, launched on March 6, 2025. Designed to bridge human intent and actionable outcomes, Manus AI leverages advanced models like Claude 3.5 Sonnet and Alibaba's Qwen, combined with a "CodeAct" approach using executable Python code, to autonomously plan, execute, and refine complex research tasks.

Unlike traditional tools that require manual input at every step, Manus AI operates as a multi-agent system, delegating tasks to specialized sub-agents to streamline methodology development for graduate students in MS, MBA, M.Tech, M.Phil, LLM, Ph.D., D.Sc., and D.Litt. programs. Its ability to process multi-modal data (text, images, code) and integrate with tools like web browsers and databases makes it a powerful ally for crafting rigorous methodology sections.

The platform's strength lies in its autonomous execution of research workflows, from literature analysis to hypothesis generation and experimental design, significantly reducing the time and effort required compared to traditional methods. With features like iterative task refinement, real-time web scraping, and data visualization, Manus AI excels at synthesizing methodological insights and proposing tailored research designs. Currently in invitation-only beta, it offers a glimpse into the future of agentic AI, with users praising its ability to handle complex tasks like academic research autonomously. By integrating Manus AI, students can craft methodology sections that are innovative, data-driven, and aligned with their research

Manus AI outperforms traditional methods by:

- **Autonomy:** Independently plans and executes research tasks, reducing manual effort compared to traditional literature reviews and design planning.
- **Multi-Modal Processing:** Handles text, images, and code, enabling comprehensive analysis of methodological literature and data visualizations.
- **Tool Integration:** Seamlessly connects with browsers, code editors, and databases for real-time data retrieval and analysis, streamlining workflow design.
- **Iterative Refinement:** Adapts workflows based on new data, ensuring methodologies remain relevant and robust.

- **Scalability:** Processes large datasets and complex tasks, ideal for interdisciplinary or data-intensive methodologies.

Manus AI's features are tailored for methodology development:

- **Autonomous Literature Analysis:** Scans and synthesizes methodological papers, extracting study designs, data

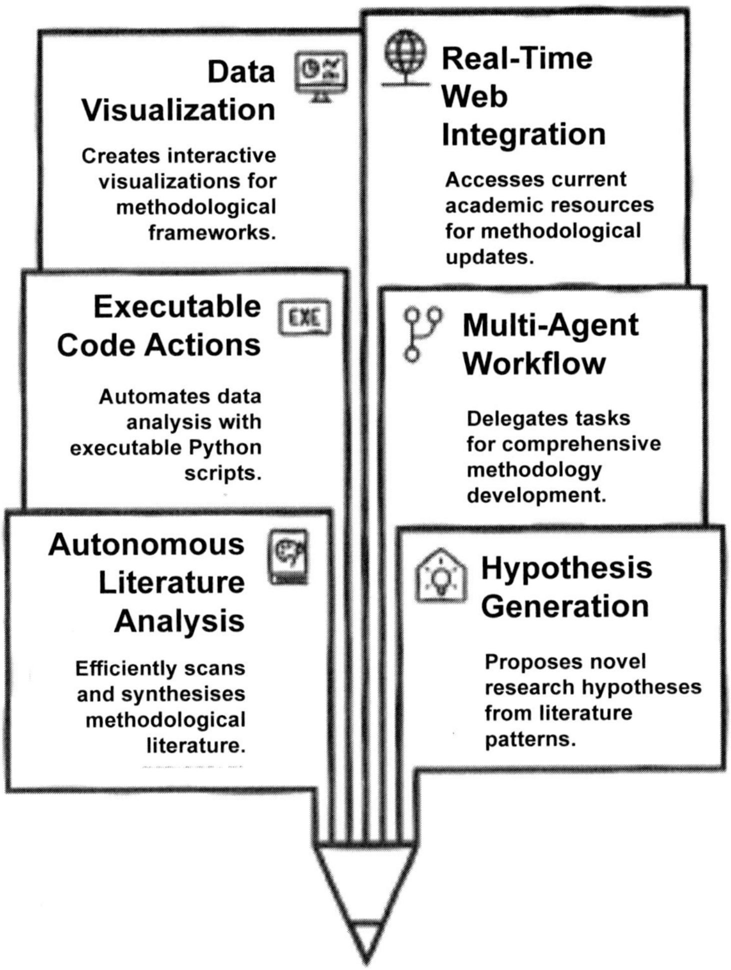

Manus AI Core Features Toolkit

collection methods, and analytical frameworks using web scraping and database access.

- **Hypothesis Generation:** Proposes research hypotheses based on literature patterns, supporting novel methodological approaches.
- **Executable Code Actions ("CodeAct"):** Generates and runs Python scripts to automate data analysis or experimental design, enhancing methodological precision.
- **Multi-Agent Workflow:** Delegates tasks to specialized sub-agents (e.g., data retrieval, analysis, visualization), ensuring comprehensive methodology development.
- **Data Visualization:** Creates charts, tables, and interactive dashboards to illustrate methodological frameworks or data analysis plans.
- **Real-Time Web Integration:** Accesses academic databases and websites to retrieve up-to-date methodological resources, ensuring currency.
- **Collaborative Feedback:** Allows sharing of outputs with advisors for iterative refinement, maintaining academic rigor.

To craft a strong methodology section with Manus AI:

- **Step 1: Access Platform:** Join the invitation-only beta via manus.im, outlining your research use case to secure access.
- **Step 2: Define Task:** Input a prompt (e.g., "Design a mixed-methods study for AI ethics research") to initiate autonomous workflow.
- **Step 3: Analyze Literature:** Upload papers or let Manus AI scrape academic databases to extract methodologies and propose designs.
- **Step 4: Generate Workflow:** Review AI-generated methodological frameworks, including data collection and analysis plans, with visualizations.

- **Step 5: Refine and Validate:** Share outputs with advisors via Manus's collaborative features, cross-checking with primary sources for accuracy.

Advanced Techniques

- **Interdisciplinary Design:** Use Manus AI to synthesize methods from multiple fields, creating hybrid methodologies for novel research.
- **Data-Driven Hypotheses:** Leverage hypothesis generation to propose innovative research designs based on literature patterns.
- **Automated Analysis:** Use CodeAct to run statistical analyses or simulations, embedding results in your methodology section.
- **Collaborative Iteration:** Share visualizations and drafts with peers via Manus Spaces for feedback, refining complex workflows.

Pro Tip

Input a detailed prompt (e.g., "Design a qualitative methodology with interview protocols for studying renewable energy policies") and use Manus AI's visualization tools to create methodological diagrams. Pair with Paperpal to polish the draft, ensuring a rigorous, professional methodology section that impresses examiners.

By adopting Manus AI, students can craft a methodology section that is faster, data-driven, and innovative. Apply for beta access at manus.im to streamline your research design and elevate your thesis to new heights of scholarly excellence.

In Conclusion, Chapter 3 has showcased the transformative power of AI tools in revolutionizing methodology development for graduate students in MS, MBA, M.Tech, M.Phil, LLM,

Ph.D., D.Sc., and D.Litt. programs. With over 3 million scholarly articles published annually as of June 2025, crafting a rigorous methodology section is a daunting task, requiring analysis of vast literature and alignment of study designs with research objectives. Tools like Thesis AI, Scholarcy, NotebookLM, SciSummary, and Manus AI streamline this process, offering unparalleled efficiency and precision. These platforms automate literature summarization, propose tailored research designs, and organize workflows, enabling students to develop methodologies that are robust, innovative, and evidence-based.

- **Thesis AI** stands out for synthesizing up to 100 papers into LaTeX-formatted methodology drafts with precise citations, ideal for technical theses requiring structured designs.
- **Scholarcy** accelerates literature analysis with smart summaries and comparative matrices, pinpointing methodological gaps and supporting diverse learners with accessible formats.
- **NotebookLM** organizes research protocols through conversational querying and interactive notebooks, generating timelines and outlines to align methods with goals.
- **SciSummary** processes large literature sets, extracting methodologies from figures and text in minutes, perfect for rapid, comprehensive design synthesis.
- **Manus AI** redefines methodology development with autonomous task execution, generating data-driven frameworks and visualizations for complex, interdisciplinary research.

To maximize impact, integrate these tools strategically: leverage Scholarcy and SciSummary for quick summarization, NotebookLM for workflow organization, Thesis AI for structured drafting, and Manus AI for innovative designs. Validate AI outputs with primary sources and advisor feedback to ensure rigor, and document tool usage transparently to uphold academic integrity. Pair with Paperpal (from Chapter 2) to polish drafts, ensuring clarity and scholarly tone. These tools save hours, enhance methodological precision, and position your research for impact.

Act now to transform your methodology section. Start with SciSummary or Scholarcy to analyze literature, use NotebookLM to structure workflows, draft with Thesis AI, and innovate with Manus AI. Experiment with one tool today, build a tailored workflow, and craft a methodology that drives a groundbreaking thesis. Your research can shape your field—harness these AI tools to make it happen.

Chapter 4

Data Analysis and Results Presentation

The data analysis and results presentation section is a cornerstone for graduate students across diverse academic programs, as it converts complex datasets into clear, evidence-based findings that directly address research objectives. This critical phase requires precise data processing, advanced analytical techniques, and impactful visualizations, all tightly aligned with the thesis's methodological framework. Traditionally, this process demands weeks of manual effort—cleaning datasets, conducting intricate statistical or qualitative analyses, and designing charts or tables—often with risks of errors due to the volume and complexity of data, particularly in interdisciplinary or data-intensive studies.

AI-powered tools transform this process by automating data analysis, enhancing methodological rigor, and streamlining the creation of compelling visualizations, enabling students to produce robust results efficiently. Platforms like SciSpace, Julius AI, Claude, Gemini Advanced AI, and Elicit provide specialized capabilities tailored for academic research, from statistical processing to dynamic charts and narrative generation. These tools tackle repetitive tasks such as data cleaning, pattern identification, and initial visualization, allowing researchers to focus on interpreting results and crafting persuasive arguments. Key benefits include:

- **Speed and Efficiency:** Automate data processing and analysis, reducing weeks of work to hours, enabling faster iteration and refinement.

- **Precision and Depth:** Leverage AI algorithms to detect subtle patterns and ensure accurate statistical or qualitative outputs, minimizing human error.
- **Visual Impact:** Generate professional-grade charts, graphs, and tables, enhancing the clarity and persuasiveness of results presentation.
- **Scalability:** Handle large, complex datasets across disciplines, ideal for interdisciplinary research requiring diverse analytical approaches.
- **Academic Alignment:** Ensure outputs meet scholarly standards, with tools designed to integrate seamlessly with thesis workflows.

Success in this phase hinges on integrating AI efficiency with human expertise. While AI excels at processing vast datasets and creating visualizations, researchers must validate results, ensure ethical compliance, and contextualize findings within their study's framework. This chapter explores how SciSpace, Julius AI, Claude, Gemini Advanced AI, and Elicit empower students to craft a data analysis and results section that is rigorous, clear, and impactful. Start leveraging these tools today to streamline your workflow, deepen analytical insights, and present findings that elevate your thesis's scholarly impact.

4.1 SciSpace: AI-Driven Literature-Integrated Data Analysis and Visualization

SciSpace, accessible at scispace.com, is an AI-powered research platform that revolutionizes data analysis and results presentation for graduate students in MS, MBA, M.Tech, M.Phil, LLM, Ph.D., D.Sc., and D.Litt. programs. Leveraging advanced natural language processing (NLP) and a database of over 280 million research papers, SciSpace integrates literature insights with robust data analysis tools, enabling students to process datasets, conduct statistical or qualitative analyses, and generate professional-grade visualizations efficiently.

Unlike traditional methods that require manual data processing in tools like Excel or SPSS and time-intensive visualization design, SciSpace automates these tasks, reducing weeks of work to hours while ensuring academic rigor. Its intuitive interface, combined with features like data extraction, visualization generation, and seamless integration with tools like Zotero, makes SciSpace an essential tool for crafting compelling, evidence-based results sections in theses.

The platform's strength lies in its ability to combine literature-derived insights with data analysis, enabling students to contextualize findings within existing research. SciSpace's Copilot AI, for example, allows users to upload datasets or PDFs and query specific analytical methods or visualization techniques, while its visualization tools produce charts, graphs, and tables tailored to academic standards. With a freemium model offering limited features (e.g., 10,000 words monthly) and premium plans starting at $8.34/month (yearly) or $14.30/month (monthly), SciSpace is accessible to students on varying budgets. Trusted by over 1 million researchers worldwide, including those at top universities, SciSpace streamlines the data analysis process, enhances precision, and elevates the visual impact of results, ensuring theses meet scholarly expectations.

SciSpace outperforms traditional methods in several ways:

- **Speed and Efficiency:** Automates data cleaning, analysis, and visualization, cutting processing time from days to minutes compared to manual tools like Excel or R.
- **Literature Integration:** Links analysis to relevant studies from its 280 million-paper database, ensuring results are grounded in scholarly context, unlike isolated traditional analyses.

- **Visual Impact:** Generates professional-grade charts, graphs, and tables, surpassing the manual design capabilities of tools like Tableau.
- **Scalability:** Handles large, complex datasets across disciplines, ideal for interdisciplinary research requiring diverse analytical approaches.
- **Accessibility:** Offers a user-friendly interface and Chrome extension, with features like text-to-speech for neurodivergent students, making data analysis more inclusive.

SciSpace's Features for Data Analysis and Results Presentation:

- **Data Extraction and Analysis:** Upload datasets or PDFs to extract key data points (e.g., statistical metrics, qualitative themes) and perform analyses using AI-driven algorithms, supporting both quantitative (e.g., regression) and qualitative (e.g., thematic coding) methods.
- **Visualization Generation:** Creates customizable charts (e.g., bar, line, scatter), graphs, and tables, exportable to Word, LaTeX, or PDF, ensuring publication-ready formats.
- **Copilot AI Queries:** Allows users to ask specific questions (e.g., "What statistical methods suit this dataset?" or "Generate a bar chart for these results"), delivering tailored analytical insights and visualizations.
- **Literature-Linked Analysis:** Integrates analysis with relevant papers, suggesting methodologies or benchmarks from its database to contextualize findings.
- **Multi-Format Compatibility:** Processes datasets in CSV, Excel, or PDF formats, with bulk analysis capabilities for comparing multiple datasets.
- **Reference Management:** Integrates with Zotero to manage citations for literature-linked results, ensuring accurate referencing in APA, MLA, or Chicago styles.

- **Exportable Outputs:** Exports visualizations and analysis summaries to Word, LaTeX, or CSV, streamlining integration into thesis drafts.

Characteristic	Description
Data Extraction and Analysis	AI-driven algorithms for quantitative and qualitative methods
Visualization Generation	Customizable charts, graphs, and tables for publication
Copilot AI Queries	Tailored analytical insights and visualizations via quations
Literature-Linked Analysis	Methodologies or benchmarks suggested from database
Multi-Format Compatibility	Processes datasets in CSV, Excel, or PDF formats
Reference Management	Integrates with Zotero for accurate citations
Exportable Outputs	Exports visualizations and analysis summaries to various formats

Scispace Features for Data Analysis

Comparison to Traditional Methods: Traditional data analysis and results presentation involve labor-intensive tasks: cleaning datasets in Excel, running analyses in SPSS or R, and designing visualizations in Tableau or PowerPoint. These processes can take weeks, risk errors (e.g., misinterpreting statistical outputs), and often produce basic visuals that lack academic polish. SciSpace offers:

- **Time Savings:** Analyzes datasets and generates visualizations in minutes, compared to hours or days manually.
- **Enhanced Accuracy:** Uses AI algorithms to minimize errors in data cleaning and statistical analysis, unlike manual methods prone to oversight.
- **Professional Visuals:** Produces publication-ready charts and tables, surpassing the quality of manual designs in Excel or PowerPoint.
- **Contextual Depth:** Links results to literature insights, unlike standalone traditional analyses that require separate literature reviews.
- **Scalability:** Processes large or interdisciplinary datasets effortlessly, unlike manual tools that struggle with complexity.

To Craft a Strong Results Section with SciSpace:

- **Upload Data:** Import datasets (CSV, Excel, or PDF) or relevant papers via SciSpace's dashboard or Chrome extension.
- **Analyze Data:** Use Copilot to select analysis methods (e.g., "Run a regression analysis on this dataset") and extract key metrics or themes.
- **Generate Visualizations:** Request specific visualizations (e.g., "Create a bar chart for variable X") and customize styles to match thesis requirements.

- **Integrate Literature:** Query Copilot to link results to relevant studies (e.g., "Find papers using similar statistical methods") for contextualization.
- **Export and Refine:** Export visualizations and analysis summaries to Word or LaTeX, integrating with Zotero for citations, and refine outputs to align with your thesis framework.

Best Practices for Student Adoption

- **Curate Relevant Data:** Upload clean, well-structured datasets to ensure accurate AI-driven analysis, avoiding irrelevant or noisy data.
- **Use Specific Queries:** Ask precise questions via Copilot (e.g., "Generate a scatter plot for these variables" or "Suggest qualitative coding for interview data") to tailor outputs.
- **Leverage Free Tier:** Start with the free plan's 10,000-word limit for initial analysis, upgrading to premium for large datasets or advanced visualizations.
- **Validate Outputs:** Cross-check AI-generated analyses and visualizations with raw data or advisor feedback to ensure accuracy and rigor.
- **Integrate with Workflow:** Pair SciSpace with NotebookLM (Chapter 3) for organizing analysis workflows or Paperpal (Chapter 2) for polishing result narratives.
- **Explore Accessibility Features:** Use text-to-speech or adjustable text sizes for inclusive analysis, especially for neurodivergent students or non-native speakers.
- **Document AI Use:** Transparently note SciSpace's role in your methodology to uphold academic integrity, as advised in Chapter 3.

Advanced Techniques

- **Interdisciplinary Analysis:** Combine datasets from multiple fields (e.g., biology and sociology) to generate hybrid visualizations, leveraging SciSpace's literature database.
- **Dynamic Dashboards:** Create interactive charts for advisor presentations, exportable as HTML for dynamic thesis supplements.
- **Iterative Analysis:** Run multiple analyses with varied methods (e.g., different statistical models) to identify the most robust results.
- **Collaborative Review:** Share visualizations and analysis summaries with advisors via SciSpace's export tools for real-time feedback.

User feedback highlights SciSpace's efficiency in data analysis and visualization, with one Ph.D. student noting it "saved hours by generating charts and linking results to papers instantly". However, some users report occasional oversimplification in AI summaries, requiring manual validation for nuanced datasets, and performance lags with large files. SciSpace's integration with Zotero and its Chrome extension make it a seamless addition to academic workflows, but students should verify statistical outputs for complex analyses.

By adopting SciSpace, students can craft a results section that is faster, more precise, and visually impactful. Start today at scispace.com to streamline your data analysis, enhance scholarly rigor, and elevate your thesis's academic excellence.

4.2 Julius AI: Advanced Statistical Analysis and Visualization

Julius AI, accessible at julius.ai, is a cutting-edge AI-powered platform designed to streamline data analysis and results presentation for graduate students in MS, MBA, M.Tech, M.Phil, LLM, Ph.D., D.Sc., and D.Litt. programs. Specializing in advanced statistical analysis and visualization, Julius AI leverages natural language processing (NLP) to make complex analytical techniques accessible to researchers without extensive programming or statistical expertise.

Unlike traditional tools like SPSS or R, which require steep learning curves and manual coding, Julius AI automates data processing, statistical testing, and visualization generation, reducing days of work to minutes while ensuring academic rigor. With support for multiple data formats (e.g., spreadsheets, databases, text files) and features like automated report generation, Julius AI empowers students to produce precise, publication-ready results sections that align with disciplinary standards.

The platform's strength lies in its natural language interface, allowing users to query datasets conversationally (e.g., "Run a regression on this data" or "Show me a histogram of variable X"), eliminating the need for coding skills. Julius AI's ability to generate sophisticated visualizations, conduct comprehensive statistical analyses, and produce formatted reports makes it ideal for crafting compelling, evidence-based results sections. Its freemium model offers limited analysis for free, with premium plans starting at $17/month (as of June 2025), providing affordable access for students. Trusted by researchers across disciplines, Julius AI transforms data analysis into an efficient, user-friendly process, ensuring theses meet scholarly expectations with professional-grade outputs.

Julius AI outperforms traditional methods in several ways:

- **Accessibility:** Enables complex analyses via natural language queries, unlike traditional tools requiring coding expertise (e.g., R, Python).

- **Speed and Efficiency:** Automates data cleaning, statistical testing, and visualization, cutting analysis time from hours to minutes compared to manual SPSS workflows.
- **Visual Impact:** Generates publication-quality charts and graphs tailored to data characteristics, surpassing manual designs in Excel or Tableau.
- **Comprehensive Analysis:** Supports descriptive, inferential, and advanced statistical techniques, ensuring robust results without specialized training.
- **Scalability:** Handles diverse data formats and large datasets, ideal for interdisciplinary research requiring flexible analytical approaches.

Julius AI's Features for Data Analysis and Results Presentation:

- **Natural Language Data Queries:** Allows users to analyze data by asking questions in plain language (e.g., "What's the correlation between these variables?"), delivering tailored statistical outputs and interpretations.
- **Automated Visualization:** Generates charts (e.g., bar, line, scatter, histograms), graphs, and tables based on data characteristics and research objectives, customizable for academic formats.
- **Statistical Analysis:** Provides comprehensive tools for descriptive statistics (e.g., mean, median), inferential testing (e.g., t-tests, ANOVA), and advanced methods (e.g., regression, clustering), with automated interpretation.
- **Report Generation:** Creates formatted analytical reports including findings, methods, statistical results, and visualizations, exportable to Word, PDF, or LaTeX for thesis integration.
- **Multi-Format Data Support:** Processes data in CSV, Excel, SQL databases, and text files, enabling flexible analysis across quantitative and qualitative datasets.

- **Data Cleaning Automation:** Identifies and corrects outliers, missing values, and inconsistencies, streamlining data preparation.
- **Integration with Workflow Tools:** Exports results to reference managers like Zotero or editing tools like Paperpal for seamless thesis workflows.

Comparison to Traditional Methods: Traditional data analysis involves manual data cleaning in Excel, statistical testing in SPSS or R, and visualization design in Tableau or PowerPoint, often taking days and risking errors due to complex coding or misinterpretation. Julius AI offers:

- **Time Savings:** Completes analysis and visualization in minutes, compared to hours or days with traditional tools.

To Craft a Strong Results Section with Julius AI

- **Upload Data:** Import datasets (CSV, Excel, or text) via Julius AI's dashboard, ensuring data is structured for analysis.
- **Explore Data:** Use natural language queries (e.g., "Show descriptive statistics for this dataset") to identify patterns, outliers, and relationships.
- **Conduct Statistical Analysis:** Query specific tests (e.g., "Run a linear regression on variables X and Y") and review AI-generated results, including p-values and interpretations.
- **Generate Visualizations:** Request charts or graphs (e.g., "Create a scatter plot for these results") and customize styles to meet academic standards.
- **Export Reports:** Generate and export comprehensive reports with findings, visualizations, and methods to Word or LaTeX, integrating with Zotero for citations.

- **Ease of Use:** Eliminates coding barriers with natural language queries, unlike R's syntax-heavy workflows.
- **Error Reduction:** Automates data cleaning and statistical validation, minimizing human errors common in manual analysis.
- **Professional Outputs:** Produces polished visualizations and reports, surpassing the quality of manual designs in Excel or SPSS.
- **Holistic Workflow:** Combines analysis, visualization, and reporting in one platform, unlike fragmented traditional processes.

Best Practices for Student Adoption

- **Curate Clean Data:** Upload well-organized datasets to ensure accurate AI-driven analysis, addressing missing values upfront.
- **Use Precise Queries:** Frame specific questions (e.g., "Perform an ANOVA on these groups" or "Generate a pie chart for this data") to optimize outputs.
- **Leverage Free Tier:** Start with the free plan for initial exploration, upgrading to premium ($17/month) for large datasets or advanced analyses.
- **Validate Outputs:** Cross-check statistical results and visualizations with raw data or advisor feedback to ensure accuracy and rigor.
- **Integrate with Workflow:** Pair Julius AI with SciSpace for literature-linked visualizations or Paperpal for polishing report narratives.
- **Document AI Use:** Note Julius AI's role in your methodology transparently to maintain academic integrity, as advised in Chapter 3.
- **Optimize Visuals:** Customize visualizations to align with disciplinary norms (e.g., APA-style tables for psychology, detailed graphs for engineering).

Advanced Techniques

- **Multi-Method Analysis:** Run multiple statistical tests (e.g., regression followed by clustering) to validate findings from different angles.
- **Interdisciplinary Visualizations:** Create hybrid visualizations (e.g., combining quantitative graphs with qualitative summaries) for mixed-methods research.
- **Presentation Optimization:** Generate multiple visualization formats (e.g., static charts for thesis, interactive plots for presentations) for diverse audiences.
- **Automated Reporting:** Use report generation to create supplementary materials (e.g., appendices with detailed statistical outputs) for robust theses.

User feedback praises Julius AI for its "intuitive interface that makes stats accessible to non-coders" and its "fast, accurate visualizations". Some users note occasional limitations in handling highly specialized statistical models (e.g., Bayesian analysis), suggesting manual validation for niche methods. Its affordability and multi-format support make it a top choice for students seeking efficient, professional-grade results presentation.

By adopting Julius AI, students can craft a results section that is faster, more precise, and visually compelling. Start today at julius.ai to streamline your data analysis, enhance scholarly rigor, and elevate your thesis's academic excellence.

4.3 Claude AI: Narrative Generation and Qualitative Data Analysis

Claude AI, developed by Anthropic and accessible at claude.ai, is a powerful conversational AI tool designed to enhance data analysis and results presentation, particularly for qualitative and mixed-methods research. Tailored for graduate students in MS, MBA, M.Tech, M.Phil, LLM, Ph.D., D.Sc., and D.Litt. programs, Claude's natural language processing (NLP) capabilities and built-in Analysis Tool enable it to process datasets, generate insightful narratives, and create interactive visualizations with a focus on ethical AI use.

Unlike traditional qualitative analysis tools like NVivo, which require manual coding and extensive training, Claude automates thematic analysis, sentiment detection, and narrative synthesis, reducing weeks of work to hours while maintaining academic rigor. Its JavaScript-based Analysis Tool, available to all users (with enhanced features for Pro users at $20/month), supports data processing and visualization, making it ideal for crafting compelling, narrative-driven results sections in theses.

Claude's strength lies in its ability to generate coherent, contextually rich narratives from qualitative data (e.g., interviews, surveys) and support quantitative analysis through its Analysis Tool, introduced in October 2024. By processing data in formats like CSV, Excel, and JSON, and running JavaScript code in a browser-based sandbox, Claude delivers precise, reproducible results and interactive visualizations (e.g., bar charts, line graphs). Its emphasis on ethical AI, including bias detection and transparent outputs, ensures alignment with academic standards. Trusted by researchers for its natural, human-like responses, Claude streamlines qualitative analysis and visualization, making it accessible to students without advanced technical skills.

Claude outperforms traditional methods in several ways:

- **Ease of Use:** Natural language queries simplify complex qualitative and quantitative analysis, unlike NVivo's manual coding or SPSS's coding-heavy workflows.
- **Narrative Generation:** Produentionally synthesizes qualitative findings into coherent narratives, surpassing manual thematic analysis in speed and clarity.

- **Visualization Capabilities:** Generates interactive, publication-ready visualizations via JavaScript, outperforming static charts from tools like Excel.
- **Ethical Compliance:** Includes built-in bias detection and transparent reporting, addressing concerns often overlooked in traditional methods.
- **Versatility:** Handles both qualitative (e.g., text analysis) and quantitative (e.g., statistical summaries) data, ideal for mixed-methods research.

Claude AI's Features for Data Analysis and Results Presentation:

- **Natural Language Queries:** Enables users to analyze data by asking conversational questions (e.g., "Identify themes in these interview transcripts" or "Create a bar chart for this CSV"), eliminating coding requirements.
- **Qualitative Analysis:** Performs thematic analysis, sentiment detection, and narrative synthesis on text-based data (e.g., interviews, open-ended surveys), generating structured summaries.
- **Analysis Tool (JavaScript Sandbox):** Runs JavaScript to process datasets (up to 30MB), conduct statistical calculations (e.g., descriptive stats, correlations), and create interactive visualizations.
- **Visualization Generation:** Produces charts (e.g., bar, line, pie, scatter) and dashboards via Artifacts, customizable for academic formats and interactive for advisor presentations.
- **Report Generation:** Creates formatted reports with findings, visualizations, and interpretations, exportable to Word, PDF, or TypeScript for thesis integration.
- **Multi-Format Data Support:** Processes CSV, Excel, JSON, and text files, supporting diverse datasets from qualitative interviews to quantitative surveys.

- **Ethical Safeguards:** Detects potential biases in outputs and provides transparent explanations of analysis steps, ensuring academic integrity.

Comparison to Traditional Methods: Traditional qualitative analysis involves manual coding in NVivo or MAXQDA, while quantitative analysis requires tools like SPSS or R, both demanding significant time and expertise. These methods risk human error, lack integration, and produce static outputs. Claude offers:

- **Time Savings:** Automates thematic coding and statistical analysis, reducing processing time from days to minutes compared to NVivo or SPSS.

To Craft a Strong Results Section with Claude AI

- **Upload Data:** Import datasets (CSV, Excel, JSON, or text) via Claude's dashboard, ensuring files are under 30MB.
- **Explore Data:** Use natural language queries (e.g., "Summarize themes in these interview responses" or "Calculate descriptive stats for this CSV") to identify patterns or metrics.
- **Conduct Analysis:** Query specific analyses (e.g., "Perform a sentiment analysis on survey responses" or "Run a correlation on variables X and Y") and review AI-generated outputs.
- **Generate Visualizations:** Request visualizations (e.g., "Create a line graph for sales trends" or "Show a pie chart of response categories") and customize via Artifacts for academic formats.
- **Export Reports:** Generate and export reports with narratives, visualizations, and methods to Word or PDF, integrating with Zotero for citations.

- **Accessibility:** Eliminates coding barriers with natural language interfaces, unlike R's syntax-heavy environment.
- **Narrative Coherence:** Generates polished, contextually rich narratives, surpassing manual qualitative synthesis in clarity and speed.
- **Interactive Visuals:** Creates dynamic, interactive charts via Artifacts, outperforming static Excel or Tableau visuals.
- **Integrated Workflow:** Combines qualitative and quantitative analysis in one platform, unlike fragmented traditional tools.

Best Practices for Student Adoption

- **Prepare Clean Data:** Ensure datasets are well-structured (e.g., consistent headers, no missing values) to optimize Claude's analysis accuracy.
- **Use Specific Prompts:** Frame precise queries (e.g., "Identify key themes in these focus group transcripts" or "Generate a scatter plot for this dataset") for tailored outputs.
- **Leverage Free Tier:** Start with Claude's free plan for initial analysis, upgrading to Pro ($20/month) for larger datasets or advanced features.
- **Validate Outputs:** Cross-check qualitative narratives and statistical results with raw data or advisor feedback to ensure rigor, addressing potential hallucinations.
- **Integrate with Workflow:** Pair Claude with SciSpace (Section 4.1) for literature-linked visuals or Paperpal (Chapter 2) for narrative polishing, as recommended in Chapter 3.
- **Document AI Use:** Transparently note Claude's role in your methodology to uphold academic integrity, per Chapter 3's guidance.

- **Address Bias:** Use Claude's bias detection to review qualitative outputs, ensuring fairness in narrative interpretations.

Advanced Techniques

- **Mixed-Methods Analysis:** Combine qualitative (e.g., thematic summaries) and quantitative (e.g., statistical correlations) outputs for interdisciplinary research.
- **Interactive Dashboards:** Create dynamic dashboards via Artifacts for advisor presentations, adjusting variables interactively.
- **Iterative Refinement:** Refine outputs with follow-up prompts (e.g., "Add data labels to this chart" or "Explain this theme in more detail") for precision.
- **Model Comparison:** Query Claude to compare statistical models (e.g., "Compare linear regression vs. decision tree for this dataset") for robust analysis.

> **Pro Tip**
>
> Prompt Claude with "Generate a narrative summary of these interview themes and a bar chart of response frequencies, formatted for APA publication" to create a cohesive results section. Pair with Paperpal for polished narratives and SciSpace for literature integration, ensuring a rigorous, visually compelling thesis chapter.

User feedback highlights Claude's "slick user experience" and "sophisticated contextual understanding" for qualitative analysis and visualizations, though some note limitations with large datasets (>30MB) and occasional inaccuracies in complex math. Its JavaScript-based Analysis Tool and ethical focus make it a standout for narrative-driven and mixed-methods research, but students should validate outputs for specialized analyses.

By adopting Claude AI, students can craft a results section that is efficient, narrative-rich, and visually impactful. Start today at claude.ai to streamline your data analysis, ensure ethical compliance, and elevate your thesis's academic excellence.

4.4 Gemini Advanced AI: Versatile Data Analysis and Visualization

Gemini Advanced AI, accessible via gemini.google.com, is a powerful, multimodal AI platform powered by Google's Gemini 2.5 Pro model, designed to enhance data analysis and results presentation for graduate students in MS, MBA, M.Tech, M.Phil, LLM, Ph.D., D.Sc., and D.Litt. programs. Leveraging advanced reasoning, a 1-million-token context window, and integration with Google Workspace (e.g., Docs, Sheets), Gemini Advanced excels at processing diverse data types (text, images, CSV, Excel) and generating interactive visualizations and reports.

Unlike traditional tools like Tableau or Excel, which require manual design and technical expertise, Gemini Advanced automates data analysis, visualization, and narrative synthesis through natural language queries, reducing hours of work to minutes. Its Deep Research feature and compatibility with tools like NotebookLM (Chapter 3) make it ideal for crafting robust, visually compelling results sections in theses.

Gemini Advanced's versatility lies in its ability to handle both quantitative and qualitative data, supporting tasks from statistical analysis to thematic synthesis. Available through Google AI Pro (free for students through June 2026 with 2TB storage) or Ultra plans ($20/month), it offers high usage limits and features like Deep Research for literature-linked analysis. Posts on X praise its data analysis capabilities, noting its ability to "analyze Excel files and create charts without formulas" and its edge over competitors in product ideation. With privacy certifications (e.g., ISO 42001, SOC 1/2/3) and ethical safeguards, Gemini Advanced ensures secure, academically rigorous outputs, making it a top choice for students seeking efficiency and impact.

Gemini Advanced outperforms traditional methods in several ways:

- **Multimodal Flexibility:** Processes text, images, and datasets, unlike Tableau's focus on structured data or NVivo's qualitative-only scope.
- **Speed and Automation:** Completes complex analyses and visualizations in minutes, compared to hours or days with manual tools like SPSS or Excel.
- **Interactive Visuals:** Generates dynamic charts and dashboards, surpassing static outputs from traditional software.
- **Literature Integration:** Uses Deep Research to contextualize findings with web-sourced literature, unlike isolated traditional analyses.
- **Accessibility:** Simplifies analysis via natural language, eliminating coding barriers present in R or Python.

Gemini Advanced AI's Features for Data Analysis and Results Presentation:

- **Natural Language Queries:** Allows conversational data analysis (e.g., "Analyze this CSV for trends" or "Summarize themes in these survey responses"), accessible to non-technical users.
- **Data Analysis:** Supports statistical analysis (e.g., descriptive stats, correlations) and qualitative synthesis (e.g., thematic coding), processing up to 1,500 pages of data.

- **Visualization Generation:** Creates interactive charts (e.g., bar, line, bubble, scatter) and dashboards via Canvas, customizable for academic formats.
- **Deep Research:** Browses hundreds of web sources to contextualize findings, generating multi-page reports with citations.
- **Report Generation:** Produces formatted reports with findings, visualizations, and interpretations, exportable to Google Docs, Word, or PDF.
- **Multi-Format Support:** Handles CSV, Excel, JSON, text, and images, supporting diverse datasets from surveys to interview transcripts.
- **Workspace Integration:** Seamlessly integrates with Google Docs, Sheets, and Slides for streamlined workflows and citation management with Zotero.

<u>**Comparison to Traditional Methods**</u>**:** Traditional data analysis and visualization involve manual workflows: cleaning data in Excel, coding in R, or designing charts in Tableau, often taking days and risking errors. Qualitative analysis in NVivo requires tedious coding, while integrating literature is a separate task. Gemini Advanced offers:

- **Time Efficiency:** Automates analysis and visualization, reducing processing time compared to manual tools.
- **Ease of Use:** Natural language queries eliminate coding needs, unlike R or SPSS's technical barriers.
- **Dynamic Outputs:** Produces interactive, publication-ready visuals, outperforming static Excel or Tableau charts.
- **Integrated Analysis:** Combines quantitative, qualitative, and literature-linked analysis in one platform, unlike fragmented traditional workflows.
- **Error Reduction:** AI-driven data cleaning and validation minimize human errors common in manual processes.

To Craft a Strong Results Section with Gemini Advanced AI:

- **Upload Data:** Import datasets (CSV, Excel, JSON, or text) or images via gemini.google.com, ensuring files are under the 1-million-token limit.
- **Explore Data:** Use queries like "Show descriptive stats for this dataset" or "Identify themes in these interview responses" to uncover patterns and insights.
- **Conduct Analysis:** Request specific analyses (e.g., "Run a correlation on variables X and Y" or "Summarize key themes in survey data") and review outputs.
- **Generate Visualizations:** Prompt for visuals (e.g., "Create a bubble chart for health indicators" or "Design a bar chart for survey results") and customize via Canvas.
- **Export Reports:** Use Deep Research to contextualize findings, then export reports and visualizations to Google Docs or Word, integrating with Zotero for citations.

Best Practices for Student Adoption

- **Curate Structured Data:** Ensure datasets are clean and organized (e.g., consistent headers, no missing values) to optimize analysis accuracy.
- **Use Precise Prompts:** Frame specific queries (e.g., "Generate a scatter plot for this dataset in APA format" or "Summarize themes from these focus groups") for tailored results.
- **Leverage Free Plan:** Use the free Google AI Pro plan for students (through June 2026) for initial analysis, upgrading to Ultra ($20/month) for advanced features.
- **Validate Outputs:** Cross-check statistical results and narratives with raw data or advisor feedback to ensure rigor, addressing potential inaccuracies.

- **Integrate with Workflow:** Pair with SciSpace (Section 4.1) for literature-linked visuals, Julius AI (Section 4.2) for statistical depth, or Paperpal (Chapter 2) for narrative polishing.
- **Document AI Use:** Transparently note Gemini's role in your methodology to uphold academic integrity, as advised in Chapter 3.
- **Use Deep Research:** Query "Research studies related to my findings" to contextualize results, ensuring scholarly depth.

Advanced Techniques

- **Mixed-Methods Analysis:** Combine quantitative stats and qualitative narratives (e.g., survey stats with interview themes) for interdisciplinary theses.
- **Interactive Dashboards:** Create dynamic dashboards via Canvas for advisor presentations, adjusting variables in real-time.
- **Iterative Refinement:** Use follow-up prompts (e.g., "Add error bars to this chart" or "Deepen this thematic summary") to enhance precision.
- **Literature-Enhanced Results:** Leverage Deep Research to benchmark findings against recent studies, strengthening academic credibility.

Pro Tip

Prompt Gemini with "Analyze this dataset for trends, generate an APA-formatted bar chart, and link findings to relevant studies" to create a robust results section. Pair with Paperpal for polished narratives and Claude for qualitative depth, ensuring a compelling, evidence-based thesis chapter.

User feedback highlights Gemini's "great data analysis capabilities" for spreadsheets and visualizations and its "thoughtful, smart" performance in complex tasks. Some note limitations in coding compared to competitors like GPT-4 and occasional inaccuracies in experimental models. Its integration with Google Workspace and free student access make it a powerful tool for academic workflows, but students should validate outputs for complex analyses.

By adopting Gemini Advanced AI, students can craft a results section that is efficient, versatile, and visually impactful. Start today at gemini.google.com to streamline your data analysis, enhance scholarly rigor, and elevate your thesis's academic excellence.

4.5 Elicit: Pattern Identification and Hypothesis Testing

Elicit, accessible at elicit.com, is an AI-powered research assistant designed to accelerate data analysis and results presentation for graduate students in MS, MBA, M.Tech, M.Phil, LLM, Ph.D., D.Sc., and D.Litt. programs. Leveraging advanced language models and a database of over 125 million academic papers from Semantic Scholar, Elicit excels at identifying patterns, testing hypotheses, and synthesizing findings from large datasets, particularly in empirical domains like biomedicine and machine learning.

Unlike traditional tools like SPSS or NVivo, which require manual data processing and extensive training, Elicit automates data extraction, summarization, and thematic synthesis, reducing weeks of work to hours. Its user-friendly interface, praised for simplicity, and integration with Zotero make it ideal for crafting rigorous, evidence-based results sections in theses.

Elicit's strength lies in its ability to process large datasets and academic papers via natural language queries (e.g., "Extract key variables from these papers" or "Identify patterns in this dataset"), delivering structured tables, summaries, and synthesized insights. Used by over 2 million researchers, it offers a free plan with unlimited searches and limited data extraction, with Plus ($10/month) and Pro ($42/month) plans for advanced features. Elicit's Systematic Review workflow achieves 99.4% accuracy in data extraction, enabling students to analyze thousands of papers efficiently. While less suited for non-empirical domains, its focus on concrete results and transparent outputs ensures academic credibility, making it a powerful tool for hypothesis-driven research.

Elicit outperforms traditional methods in several ways:

- **Efficiency:** Automates data extraction and synthesis, cutting analysis time compared to manual SPSS or Excel workflows.
- **Pattern Identification:** Detects trends and themes across large datasets and papers, surpassing manual coding in NVivo for speed and scale.
- **Data Organization:** Generates structured tables for easy comparison, unlike fragmented traditional processes.
- **Literature Integration:** Links findings to 125 million papers, providing context absent in standalone tools like R.
- **Accessibility:** Simplifies analysis with natural language, eliminating coding barriers of Python or R.

Elicit's Features for Data Analysis and Results Presentation:

- **Natural Language Queries:** Enables users to extract data or identify patterns by asking questions (e.g., "What are the main findings on heart rate interventions?"), accessible to non-technical users.

- **Data Extraction:** Automatically extracts variables (e.g., participant count, study design) from papers or uploaded datasets into organized tables, with 90% accuracy.
- **Pattern Identification:** Detects trends, correlations, and themes across datasets or papers, ideal for hypothesis testing in empirical research.
- **Thematic Synthesis:** Synthesizes findings into concise summaries, highlighting key insights across multiple sources.
- **Visualization Support:** Generates basic charts (e.g., bar, scatter) from extracted data, exportable for academic formats.
- **Systematic Review Workflow:** Screens and extracts data from thousands of papers in 80% less time, rivaling human accuracy.
- **Export and Integration:** Exports tables and summaries as CSV, RIS, or BibTeX, integrating with Zotero for seamless citation management.

Comparison to Traditional Methods: Traditional data analysis involves manual data cleaning in Excel, statistical testing in SPSS, or qualitative coding in NVivo, often requiring days of work and risking errors. Literature synthesis is a separate, time-intensive task. Elicit offers:

- **Time Savings:** Extracts and synthesizes data in minutes, compared to hours or days with manual tools.
- **Ease of Use:** Natural language queries eliminate coding needs, unlike R or Python's technical barriers.
- **Scalability:** Processes thousands of papers or large datasets, surpassing NVivo's capacity for qualitative analysis.
- **Structured Outputs:** Organizes data into tables and summaries, unlike fragmented Excel or SPSS results.

- **Accuracy:** Achieves 99.4% extraction accuracy, reducing errors common in manual processes.

To Craft a Strong Results Section with Elicit

- **Upload Data or Query Papers:** Import datasets (CSV, Excel, or PDFs) or query Elicit's 125 million-paper database with a research question (e.g., "What factors influence heart rate?").
- **Extract Data:** Use prompts like "Extract participant counts and outcomes from these papers" to generate structured tables.
- **Identify Patterns:** Query "Identify trends in this dataset" or "Synthesize findings across these studies" to detect correlations or themes.
- **Generate Visualizations:** Request basic charts (e.g., "Create a bar chart of outcome frequencies") and refine for academic formats.
- **Export Results:** Download tables, summaries, or charts as CSV or BibTeX, integrating with Zotero for citations and thesis drafts.

Best Practices for Student Adoption

- **Curate Relevant Data:** Upload clean datasets or specific PDFs to ensure accurate extraction and pattern detection.
- **Use Precise Queries:** Frame targeted prompts (e.g., "Extract study designs from these papers" or "Show correlations in this dataset") for optimal results.
- **Leverage Free Plan:** Start with the free plan for unlimited searches and limited extractions, upgrading to Plus ($10/month) for larger datasets.
- **Validate Outputs:** Cross-check extracted data and summaries with original sources to address potential inaccuracies, as Elicit may generalize themes.

- **Integrate with Workflow:** Pair with SciSpace (Section 4.1) for advanced visualizations, Julius AI (Section 4.2) for statistical depth, or Paperpal (Chapter 2) for narrative polishing, per Chapter 3's guidance.
- **Document AI Use:** Note Elicit's role in your methodology transparently to uphold academic integrity, as advised in Chapter 3.
- **Use Filters:** Apply filters (e.g., study type, publication year) to refine results for systematic reviews or meta-analyses.

Advanced Techniques

- **Systematic Reviews:** Use Elicit's Systematic Review workflow to screen and extract data from thousands of papers, saving 80% of manual effort.
- **Hypothesis Testing:** Query "Test this hypothesis across papers" to validate research questions with synthesized evidence.
- **Interdisciplinary Synthesis:** Combine datasets and papers from multiple fields (e.g., biomedicine and psychology) to identify cross-disciplinary patterns.
- **Notebook Organization:** Use Elicit's Notebook feature to track queries, tables, and insights, streamlining iterative analysis.

Pro Tip

Prompt Elicit with "Extract key outcomes from these papers, generate a bar chart, and synthesize findings in APA format" to create a robust results section. Pair with Paperpal for polished narratives and Gemini Advanced for interactive visuals, ensuring a compelling, evidence-based thesis chapter.

User feedback praises Elicit for saving "hours of manual searching" and producing "accurate data tables", with several posts noting its ability to "supercharge literature reviews". However, some users report issues with repeatability (e.g., inconsistent search results across trials) and limitations in non-empirical domains. Elicit's focus on empirical research and integration with Zotero make it a standout for hypothesis-driven analysis, but students should verify outputs for nuanced datasets.

By adopting Elicit, students can craft a results section that is efficient, pattern-rich, and academically rigorous. Start today at elicit.com to streamline your data analysis, enhance hypothesis testing, and elevate your thesis's scholarly impact.

In Conclusin, Chapter 4 has showcased the transformative power of AI tools in revolutionizing data analysis and results presentation for graduate students in MS, MBA, M.Tech, M.Phil, LLM, Ph.D., D.Sc., and D.Litt. programs. With the growing complexity of research datasets and the pressure to produce publication-ready results, traditional methods—manual data cleaning in Excel, statistical testing in SPSS, or visualization design in Tableau—are time-intensive and prone to errors. Tools like SciSpace, Julius AI, Claude AI, Gemini Advanced AI, and Elicit address these challenges by automating data processing, enhancing analytical rigor, and generating compelling visualizations, enabling students to craft results sections that are precise, evidence-based, and impactful.

SciSpace (Section 4.1) integrates literature with data analysis, leveraging its 280 million-paper database to contextualize findings and produce dynamic charts, ideal for interdisciplinary research requiring scholarly depth.

Julius AI (Section 4.2) excels in statistical analysis, offering natural language queries to automate complex tests and generate publication-quality visuals, perfect for quantitative studies.

Claude AI (Section 4.3) shines in narrative generation for qualitative data, with its JavaScript-based Analysis Tool creating interactive visualizations and ensuring ethical compliance for mixed-methods research.

Gemini Advanced AI (Section 4.4) provides versatile, multimodal analysis, combining quantitative stats, qualitative synthesis, and interactive dashboards, accessible through Google's free student plan.

Elicit (Section 4.5) specializes in pattern identification and hypothesis testing, extracting data from 125 million papers with near-human accuracy, streamlining systematic reviews and empirical analysis.

To maximize impact, integrate these tools strategically: use SciSpace and Elicit for literature-linked insights, Julius AI for statistical depth, Claude AI for narrative coherence, and Gemini Advanced AI for versatile visualizations. Combine with tools from earlier chapters, such as NotebookLM (Chapter 3) for organizing workflows or Paperpal (Chapter 2) for polishing narratives, to create a seamless analysis pipeline. Validate AI outputs against raw data and advisor feedback to ensure rigor, and address ethical considerations—such as data privacy, bias detection, and transparent AI use—to maintain academic integrity, as emphasized in Chapter 3. For example, cross-check statistical results from Julius AI or thematic summaries from Claude to avoid inaccuracies, and document tool usage in your methodology.

These AI tools save hours, enhance precision, and elevate the visual and scholarly impact of your results section. Start today by experimenting with SciSpace's free tier, querying datasets in Julius AI, or exploring Elicit's Systematic Review workflow. Build a tailored analysis pipeline that aligns with your research objectives, whether quantitative, qualitative, or mixed-methods. By harnessing SciSpace, Julius AI, Claude AI, Gemini Advanced AI, and Elicit, you can craft a results section that not only meets academic standards but also positions your thesis as a groundbreaking contribution to your field. Act now—test one tool, refine your workflow, and transform your data into compelling, evidence-based insights that drive scholarly excellence.

Chapter 5

Writing, Editing, Final Polish & References

Crafting a polished, professional, and academically rigorous thesis is a critical final step for graduate students in MS, MBA, M.Tech, M.Phil, LLM, Ph.D., D.Sc., and D.Litt. programs. This phase transforms complex research into a compelling narrative that withstands scholarly scrutiny, requiring clear synthesis of findings, structured arguments, and meticulous attention to detail. Writing, editing, and formatting a thesis demand precision in language, adherence to disciplinary standards, and accurate citation management, all while maintaining originality and impact.

Traditionally, this process is labor-intensive, often taking weeks or months to draft, revise, and polish a thesis. Students face challenges like maintaining clarity across dense academic content, avoiding unintentional plagiarism, and ensuring grammatical accuracy, especially in interdisciplinary or multilingual research. With over 3 million scholarly articles published annually as of June 2025, navigating the vast academic landscape to produce well-cited, original content can feel overwhelming.

AI-powered tools revolutionize this process by automating drafting, enhancing clarity, streamlining editing, and simplifying reference management. Platforms like Jenni, Zotero, Grammarly,

Thesify, and Writefull offer specialized capabilities to address these challenges:

- **Jenni** accelerates drafting with AI-generated text tailored to academic writing.
- **Zotero** streamlines citation management and bibliography creation.
- **Grammarly** ensures grammatical precision and style consistency.
- **Thesify** enhances academic tone and vocabulary for scholarly impact.
- **Writefull** refines language and provides context-aware suggestions for scientific writing.

These tools tackle repetitive tasks—grammar correction, citation formatting, and style optimization—freeing researchers to focus on crafting persuasive arguments and impactful conclusions. Success hinges on combining AI efficiency with human oversight to validate outputs, ensure ethical compliance (e.g., avoiding over-reliance on AI-generated text), and align content with research objectives. This chapter explores how Jenni, Zotero, Grammarly, Thesify, and Writefull empower students to write, edit, and polish their theses, delivering a final product that is clear, professional, and academically robust. Start leveraging these tools today to streamline your workflow, elevate your writing quality, and produce a thesis that stands out for its scholarly excellence.

5.1 Jenni AI: AI-Powered Academic Writing and Citation Assistant

Jenni AI, accessible at jenni.ai, is an AI-powered writing assistant tailored for graduate students in MS, MBA, M.Tech, M.Phil, LLM, Ph.D., D.Sc., and D.Litt. programs, streamlining the drafting, editing, and citation processes for academic writing. Leveraging advanced natural language processing (NLP) and a research library integration, Jenni AI helps students overcome writer's block, generate coherent drafts, and produce properly cited, publication-ready theses.

Unlike traditional writing tools like Microsoft Word, which lack AI-driven suggestions, or manual citation managers, Jenni automates content generation, in-text citations, and plagiarism checks, reducing hours of work to minutes. With over 3 million users globally and 970 million words written, Jenni has grown 481% year-over-year, reaching $5.1M ARR by April 2024, cementing its leadership in academic writing tools. Its intuitive interface and ethical design ensure students maintain control over their work, aligning with academic integrity standards.

Jenni's strength lies in its ability to generate context-aware text, suggest ideas, and manage citations across APA, MLA, Chicago, Harvard, and IEEE formats, making it ideal for crafting essays, literature reviews, and theses. The free plan offers 200 AI-generated words daily, while the Unlimited plan ($12/month yearly or $30/month monthly) provides unlimited words, PDF uploads, and advanced features like plagiarism detection. Users on X praise Jenni for "supercharging academic writing" and automating citations, though some note occasional inaccuracies in complex outputs, requiring manual review. Jenni's integration with Google Docs and Zotero streamlines workflows, making it a must-have for students seeking efficiency and scholarly rigor.

Jenni outperforms traditional methods in several ways:

- **Speed:** Generates drafts and citations in minutes, compared to hours of manual writing and referencing.

- **Accessibility:** Natural language prompts simplify content creation, unlike Word's static interface.
- **Citation Automation:** Auto-generates accurate in-text citations and bibliographies, surpassing manual tools like EndNote.
- **Originality:** Includes plagiarism detection (paid plans), ensuring academic integrity, unlike basic text editors.
- **Versatility:** Supports multiple content types (essays, theses, blogs) and 30+ languages, ideal for multilingual researchers.

Jenni AI's Features for Writing, Editing, and References:

- **AI Autocomplete:** Suggests context-aware sentences and paragraphs to accelerate drafting and overcome writer's block (e.g., "Continue this literature review on climate change").
- **Citation Management:** Automatically generates in-text citations and bibliographies in APA, MLA, Chicago, Harvard, and IEEE formats, pulling from uploaded PDFs or its research library.
- **Plagiarism Detection:** Scans up to 10,000 words/month (50,000 with additional fees) to ensure originality, critical for academic submissions.
- **Outline Builder:** Creates structured outlines for essays or theses, ensuring logical flow and coherence.
- **Paraphrasing and Rewriting:** Refines tone, clarity, and style (e.g., academic, persuasive) to meet disciplinary standards.
- **Research Engine:** Integrates with uploaded sources or web searches to suggest relevant citations and content, streamlining literature reviews.
- **Export Options:** Supports LaTeX, Word, and HTML exports for seamless integration into thesis drafts.

<u>Comparison to Traditional Methods</u>: Traditional thesis writing involves drafting in Word, manually searching Google Scholar for sources, and formatting citations in tools like EndNote, often taking days and risking errors. Editing requires manual grammar checks, and plagiarism detection demands separate software. Jenni offers:

- **Time Efficiency:** Automates drafting, editing, and citations, unlike Word's manual processes.
- **Error Reduction:** AI-driven suggestions and plagiarism checks minimize mistakes, unlike human-only editing.
- **Integrated Workflow:** Combines writing, citation, and originality checks in one platform, unlike fragmented tools.
- **User-Friendly:** Simplifies complex tasks with natural language prompts, unlike EndNote's steep learning curve.
- **Scalability:** Handles large projects like dissertations, surpassing basic editors for scope and speed.

To Craft a Polished Thesis with Jenni AI:

- **Start Drafting:** Sign up at jenni.ai (free or Unlimited plan) and input your thesis title or prompt (e.g., "Draft an introduction on renewable energy policies").
- **Generate Content:** Use AI Autocomplete to expand sections or request specific tasks (e.g., "Write a conclusion for my methodology").
- **Add Citations:** Upload PDFs or query the research engine to insert citations (e.g., "Find sources on solar energy and cite in APA").
- **Refine Prose:** Use paraphrasing tools to adjust tone or clarity, ensuring academic rigor (e.g., "Make this paragraph more formal").

- **Check Originality:** Run plagiarism detection to confirm uniqueness, then export to Word or LaTeX for final formatting.

Best Practices for Student Adoption

- **Provide Clear Prompts:** Use specific instructions (e.g., "Generate a 200-word literature review on AI ethics") for accurate outputs.
- **Validate Citations:** Cross-check AI-generated citations against original sources to ensure accuracy, as minor errors can occur.
- **Leverage Free Plan:** Start with the free 200-word daily limit to test features, upgrading to Unlimited for larger projects.
- **Integrate with Workflow:** Pair with Zotero (Section 5.2) for robust citation management or Paperpal (Chapter 2) for additional editing.
- **Maintain Integrity:** Use Jenni as an assistant, not a replacement, to avoid academic dishonesty, manually reviewing outputs.
- **Explore Multilingual Support:** Utilize 30+ language options for non-native English speakers to enhance accessibility.
- **Document AI Use:** Transparently note Jenni's role in your methodology, as advised in Chapter 3, to uphold ethical standards.

Advanced Techniques

- **Iterative Drafting:** Refine drafts by prompting Jenni to rewrite sections (e.g., "Shorten this abstract to 150 words") for conciseness.
- **Literature Review Synthesis:** Query "Summarize key findings from these PDFs" to streamline review sections.

- **Collaborative Writing:** Share drafts with advisors via Google Docs integration, incorporating feedback seamlessly.
- **Custom Citation Styles:** Adjust citations to niche formats by uploading custom templates for precision.

Pro Tip

Prompt Jenni with "Generate a 300-word discussion section on my findings with APA citations" and pair with Paperpal for final polishing and Zotero for bibliography management. This creates a cohesive, well-cited thesis section that meets academic standards.

User feedback highlights Jenni's ability to "streamline writing and citations" and its "intuitive interface" for students, though some note predictable outputs for complex topics, requiring human refinement. Compared to alternatives like Paperpal, Jenni excels in content generation but may lack advanced editing precision. Its focus on academic writing, citation automation, and plagiarism checks makes it a powerful tool, but students should review outputs to ensure originality and accuracy.

By adopting Jenni AI, students can craft a thesis that is efficient, well-structured, and academically rigorous. Start today at jenni.ai to accelerate your writing, enhance your arguments, and produce a polished, professional thesis that stands out.

5.2 Zotero: Ultimate Reference Management System

Zotero, accessible at zotero.org, is a free, open-source reference management software designed to streamline citation and bibliography creation for graduate students in MS, MBA, M.Tech,

M.Phil, LLM, Ph.D., D.Sc., and D.Litt. programs. Developed by the Corporation for Digital Scholarship and originally launched in 2006 at George Mason University, Zotero simplifies the organization, storage, and citation of research materials, supporting over 10,000 citation styles, including APA, MLA, Chicago, and IEEE.

Unlike commercial tools like EndNote, which can cost $275, Zotero offers robust functionality at no cost, with a 9.1/10 TrustRadius score and a vibrant user community of over 2 million researchers. Its browser integration, cloud syncing, and compatibility with Microsoft Word, Google Docs, and LibreOffice make it an essential tool for crafting academically rigorous theses. Posts on X praise Zotero as "the best citation management tool" for its automation and open-source ethos, though some note a learning curve for advanced features.

Zotero's strength lies in its seamless integration with web browsers (Chrome, Firefox, Safari) via the Zotero Connector, which captures metadata, PDFs, and snapshots from sources like PubMed, Google Scholar, and library catalogs with a single click. It supports collaborative workflows through shared libraries and annotates PDFs directly, surpassing tools like Mendeley in citation style support and import accuracy. The free plan includes 300MB of cloud storage, with paid options from $20/year for 2GB to $120/year for unlimited storage, making it accessible for students. Zotero's open-source nature ensures data privacy and long-term sustainability, unlike proprietary alternatives.

Zotero outperforms traditional methods in several ways:

- **Efficiency:** Automates citation and bibliography formatting, saving hours compared to manual referencing in Word.
- **Accessibility:** Free and open-source, unlike EndNote's high cost, with browser-based access via ZoteroBib (zbib.org).

- **Accuracy:** Captures metadata with 99% accuracy from major databases, reducing errors in manual entry.
- **Collaboration:** Supports shared libraries for group projects, unlike manual citation sharing.
- **Scalability:** Manages large libraries (up to 100,000+ items) with robust search and tagging, surpassing Excel-based methods.

Zotero's Features for Reference Management:

- **Reference Collection:** Captures metadata, PDFs, and snapshots from websites, library catalogs, and databases (e.g., PubMed, Google Scholar) via the Zotero Connector.
- **Citation Generation:** Auto-generates in-text citations and bibliographies in over 10,000 styles, integrating with Word, Google Docs, and LibreOffice.
- **PDF Management:** Stores and annotates PDFs, with full-text search and note-taking capabilities within the desktop app.
- **Cloud Syncing:** Syncs libraries across devices via zotero.org, with a responsive web interface and iOS/Android apps.
- **Collaboration:** Enables shared group libraries for team projects, with real-time updates and note-sharing.
- **Organization Tools:** Supports drag-and-drop collections, tags, and saved searches for efficient library management.
- **Export Options:** Exports citations in BibTeX, RIS, CSL-JSON, and more, compatible with LaTeX and Overleaf for technical disciplines.

Comparison to Traditional Methods: Manual reference management involves tracking sources in spreadsheets, formatting citations by hand, and storing PDFs in folders, risking errors and lost files. Traditional tools like EndNote require costly licenses and complex setups. Zotero offers:

- **Time Savings:** Automates metadata capture and citation formatting, unlike manual entry in Word or Excel.
- **Error Reduction:** Ensures accurate metadata and citation styles, minimizing errors compared to manual formatting.
- **Integrated Workflow:** Combines collection, annotation, and citation in one platform, unlike fragmented manual processes.
- **Cost-Effectiveness:** Free core features outshine paid tools like EndNote, with affordable storage upgrades.
- **Flexibility:** Supports diverse formats and collaborative workflows, surpassing basic tools like EasyBib.

To Craft a Well-Cited Thesis with Zotero:

- **Install Zotero:** Download the desktop app (Windows, Mac, Linux) and Zotero Connector (Chrome, Firefox, Safari) from zotero.org.
- **Collect Sources:** Click the Zotero Connector icon on websites or databases to save metadata, PDFs, and snapshots to your library.

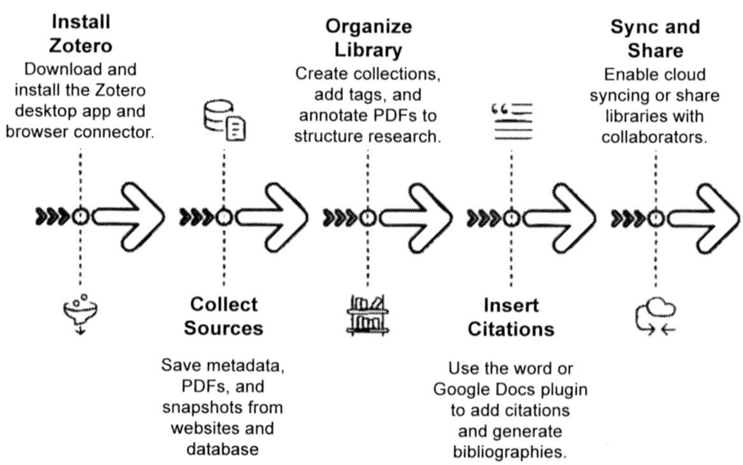

Crafting Thesisi with Zotero

- **Organize Library:** Create collections, add tags, and annotate PDFs to structure your research (e.g., by thesis chapter or topic).
- **Insert Citations:** Use the Word or Google Docs plugin to add in-text citations and generate bibliographies in your chosen style (e.g., APA, MLA).
- **Sync and Share:** Enable cloud syncing or share libraries with collaborators via zotero.org, exporting to BibTeX for LaTeX users.

Best Practices for Student Adoption

- **Start Early:** Install Zotero at the beginning of your research to streamline source collection and avoid manual tracking.
- **Use the Connector:** Pin the Zotero Connector to your browser toolbar for one-click source capture, ensuring Zotero Desktop is running.
- **Organize Effectively:** Use collections and tags (e.g., "Methodology," "Literature Review") to sort sources, leveraging Zotero's "AND" tag search for precision.
- **Leverage Free Plan:** Utilize the 300MB free storage for most projects, upgrading to paid plans only for large PDF libraries.
- **Validate Citations:** Cross-check metadata and citations against original sources to ensure accuracy, as rare import errors can occur.
- **Integrate with Workflow:** Pair with Jenni AI (Section 5.1) for drafting, Grammarly (Section 5.3) for editing, or Overleaf for LaTeX-based theses.
- **Document AI Use:** Note Zotero's role in your methodology for transparency, as advised in Chapter 3.

Advanced Techniques

- **Systematic Reviews:** Use Zotero's duplicate detection and PRISMA-compliant export options to manage large reference sets for meta-analyses.
- **Collaborative Projects:** Share group libraries with advisors or peers, using notes and tags to track feedback.
- **Custom Styles:** Install niche citation styles from Zotero's style repository or edit existing ones for journal-specific requirements.
- **PDF Annotation:** Annotate PDFs in Zotero 7's built-in reader, syncing notes across devices for efficient review.

Pro Tip

Use the Zotero Connector to capture sources from Google Scholar, then prompt Jenni AI to draft a literature review based on your Zotero library. Export citations to Word or LaTeX, and polish with Grammarly for a seamless, professional thesis.

User feedback highlights Zotero's "seamless browser integration" and "robust metadata capture", though some note compatibility issues with certain websites and a clunky interface for custom styles. Compared to Mendeley, Zotero's open-source nature and broader style support make it superior, but its 300MB free storage is lower than Mendeley's 2GB. Students should review metadata for non-English sources, as diacritics may be inconsistent. Zotero's community-driven support and free access make it a cornerstone for reference management.

By adopting Zotero, students can streamline citation workflows, ensure accuracy, and produce a polished, well-cited thesis. Start today at zotero.org to organize your research, automate citations, and elevate your academic work with ease.

5.3 Grammarly: AI-Powered Writing Enhancement

Grammarly, accessible at grammarly.com, is an AI-powered writing assistant that elevates the writing, editing, and polishing process for graduate students in MS, MBA, M.Tech, M.Phil, LLM, Ph.D., D.Sc., and D.Litt. programs. Launched in 2009,. Grammarly leverages advanced natural language processing (NLP) to enhance clarity, grammar, style, and tone, ensuring theses meet academic standards for precision and professionalism

Unlike traditional editing tools like Microsoft Word's spell-check, which offer basic corrections, Grammarly provides real-time suggestions for grammar, punctuation, style, and plagiarism detection, refining academic prose in minutes. With over 30 million daily active users and adoption by 96% of Fortune 500 companies, Grammarly is a trusted tool for academic writing. Its integration with Word, Google Docs, and browsers (Chrome, Firefox) streamlines editing workflows, making it ideal for crafting polished thesis chapters.

Grammarly's strength lies in its ability to tailor suggestions to academic writing, offering context-specific feedback on clarity, conciseness, and tone while detecting unintentional plagiarism against billions of web pages and academic sources. The free plan covers basic grammar and spelling, while Premium ($12/month yearly or $30/month monthly) and Education plans unlock advanced style suggestions, readability scores, and plagiarism checks. Several posts praise Grammarly for "transforming academic writing" and catching errors missed by human editors, though some note its suggestions can feel overly prescriptive for creative sections. Its accessibility features, like text-to-speech integration, support neurodivergent and non-native English speakers, ensuring inclusive thesis refinement.

Grammarly outperforms traditional methods in several ways:

- **Precision:** Identifies complex grammar, style, and clarity issues, surpassing Word's limited checks.
- **Speed:** Provides real-time editing suggestions, reducing hours of manual proofreading.
- **Plagiarism Detection:** Scans for unoriginal content (Premium), unlike manual checks or standalone tools like Turnitin.
- **Customization:** Tailors feedback to academic tone and specific disciplines, unlike generic editors.
- **Accessibility:** Supports 30+ languages and inclusive features, ideal for multilingual researchers.

Grammarly's Features for Writing Enhancement:

- **Grammar and Punctuation:** Corrects complex errors (e.g., subject-verb agreement, comma splices) with detailed explanations to improve writing skills.
- **Style and Clarity:** Enhances sentence structure, eliminates redundancy, and improves readability for academic prose (e.g., "Replace 'very important' with 'crucial'").
- **Plagiarism Detection:** Scans against billions of sources (Premium), flagging unoriginal text and suggesting citations to ensure academic integrity.
- **Tone Adjustment:** Aligns tone with academic standards (e.g., formal, objective) or specific audiences (e.g., examiners, journal editors).
- **Real-Time Feedback:** Integrates with Word, Google Docs, and browsers for instant suggestions during drafting.
- **Readability Scores:** Provides metrics like Flesch-Kincaid to ensure thesis accessibility for diverse readers.
- **Export Compatibility:** Saves edited documents in Word, PDF, or Google Docs formats, integrating with Zotero for citation workflows.

Comparison to Traditional Methods: Traditional editing relies on manual proofreading, Word's basic spell-check, or external editors, often taking days and missing nuanced errors. Plagiarism checks require separate tools, and style adjustments depend on subjective judgment. Grammarly offers:

- **Time Efficiency:** Automates editing and plagiarism checks, unlike manual proofreading's slow pace.
- **Comprehensive Feedback:** Addresses grammar, style, and clarity, surpassing Word's limited corrections.
- **Error Reduction:** Catches errors missed by human editors, with 96% accuracy in grammar detection.
- **Integrated Workflow:** Combines editing, tone adjustment, and plagiarism checks, unlike fragmented traditional tools.
- **Cost-Effectiveness:** Free plan suffices for basic editing, with Premium offering advanced features at a lower cost than professional editors.

To Craft a Polished Thesis with Grammarly

- **Install Grammarly**: Sign up at grammarly.com (free or Premium) and add the browser extension or desktop app for Word/Google Docs integration.
- **Upload or Draft**: Import your thesis draft or write directly in Grammarly's editor to receive real-time suggestions.
- **Refine Prose**: Accept grammar, punctuation, and style suggestions, focusing on clarity and academic tone (e.g., "Make this paragraph more formal").
- **Check Plagiarism**: Run Premium's plagiarism scan to ensure originality, addressing flagged sections with proper citations.
- **Export and Finalize**: Save edited drafts in Word or PDF, integrating with Zotero for citation formatting.

Best Practices for Student Adoption

- **Start with Free Plan:** Use basic grammar and spelling checks for initial drafts, upgrading to Premium for plagiarism detection and style refinement.
- **Customize Goals:** Set Grammarly's audience (e.g., academic) and tone (e.g., formal) to align with thesis requirements.
- **Validate Suggestions:** Review AI suggestions to avoid over-corrections, especially for discipline-specific terminology.
- **Integrate with Workflow:** Pair with Jenni AI (Section 5.1) for drafting, Zotero (Section 5.2) for citations, or Writefull (Section 5.5) for scientific polish.
- **Leverage Accessibility:** Use text-to-speech for neurodivergent students or non-native speakers to enhance comprehension.
- **Document AI Use:** Note Grammarly's role in your methodology for transparency, as advised in Chapter 3.
- **Batch Edit:** Upload full chapters to Grammarly's editor for comprehensive feedback, saving time on large documents.

Advanced Techniques

- **Discipline-Specific Editing:** Customize suggestions for fields like engineering (technical precision) or humanities (narrative flow) using domain settings.
- **Plagiarism Workflow:** Run iterative plagiarism checks during drafting to refine paraphrasing and citation practices.
- **Collaborative Editing:** Share Google Docs with advisors, using Grammarly's real-time feedback for collaborative revisions.

- **Readability Optimization:** Adjust sentences based on readability scores to ensure clarity for examiners or journal readers.

> **Pro Tip**
>
> Upload your thesis draft to Grammarly, set the tone to "Academic/Formal," and run a plagiarism check to ensure originality. Pair with Zotero for seamless citation integration and Jenni AI for drafting, creating a polished, well-cited thesis that meets scholarly standards.

User feedback lauds Grammarly for "catching errors I'd never spot" and its "intuitive interface", though some note Premium's cost and occasional overzealous suggestions for academic jargon. Compared to Writefull, Grammarly excels in general academic writing but may lack field-specific precision for STEM. Its robust plagiarism detection and real-time integration make it a cornerstone for thesis polishing, but students should manually verify suggestions for technical terms.

By adopting Grammarly, students can produce a thesis that is clear, error-free, and academically rigorous. Start today at grammarly.com to streamline your editing, enhance your prose, and elevate your thesis's scholarly impact.

5.4 Thesify: AI-Powered Academic Writing Coach

Thesify, accessible at thesify.ai, is an AI-powered academic writing assistant designed to enhance the writing process for graduate students in MS, MBA, M.Tech, M.Phil, LLM, Ph.D., D.Sc., and D.Litt. programs. Unlike generative AI tools like ChatGPT, Thesify prioritizes academic integrity by providing real-time feedback, citation assistance, and research support without writing content for users, fostering critical thinking and skill development. Developed with input from educators and universities, it supports students in producing polished essays, theses, and research papers that meet high academic standards.

With a database of over 200 million references, Thesify streamlines literature searches and ensures ethical writing practices. Its free plan offers 10 AI credits monthly (20 with a university email), with paid plans starting at $4.99/month, making it accessible for students. Several posts praise Thesify for its "thoughtful feedback" and ability to "evaluate writing like a professor", though some note its reliance on internet connectivity and limited effectiveness for niche topics .

Thesify's core strength is its AI assistant, Theo, which guides users through the writing process with structured feedback, resource suggestions, and pre-submission assessments. Unlike tools like Grammarly, which focus on grammar, Thesify evaluates argumentation, structure, and evidence, acting as a virtual writing coach. Its Agile Editor and Semantic Article Search enhance workflow efficiency, while its commitment to privacy—never using user data for AI training—ensures confidentiality . Ideal for crafting literature reviews, refining arguments, and ensuring citation accuracy, Thesify empowers students to produce high-quality, original work efficiently.

Thesify outperforms traditional methods in several ways:

- **Structured Feedback:** Provides professor-like evaluations on structure and argumentation, unlike Word's basic spell-check.
- **Time Efficiency:** Delivers instant feedback and resource suggestions, reducing hours spent on manual revisions and literature searches.

- **Ethical Design:** Promotes academic integrity by avoiding content generation, unlike ChatGPT's risk of plagiarism.
- **Research Integration:** Accesses 200 million references for relevant sources, surpassing manual Google Scholar searches.
- **User-Friendly:** Web-based platform requires no downloads, unlike complex software like EndNote.

Thesify's Features for Writing Enhancement:

- **Real-Time Feedback:** Theo provides instant suggestions on grammar, style, clarity, and argumentation, with explanations to improve writing skills (e.g., "Strengthen this claim with evidence") .
- **Semantic Article Search:** Identifies relevant academic papers from a 200 million-reference database, streamlining literature reviews.
- **Citation Assistance:** Formats citations in APA, MLA, Chicago, and other styles, ensuring accuracy and academic honesty.
- **Agile Editor:** Offers block-based editing, in-document notes, and outline creation for flexible, non-linear writing.
- **Intelligent Paper Digest:** Summarizes complex articles into concise, digestible insights to support research comprehension.
- **Pre-Submission Assessment:** Evaluates manuscript readiness, highlighting weak arguments and suggesting improvements before submission.
- **Collaboration Tools:** Supports team-based projects with shared workspaces for group assignments or advisor feedback.

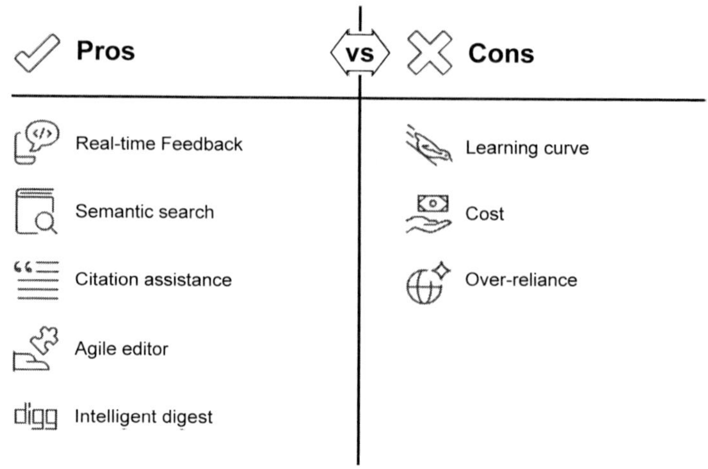

Thesify Writing Tool

<u>**Comparison to Traditional Methods**</u>**:** Traditional writing involves manual drafting in Word, searching Google Scholar for sources, and self-editing, often leading to errors and inefficiencies. Citation management requires separate tools like EndNote, and feedback depends on advisors' availability. Thesify offers:

- **Comprehensive Feedback:** Evaluates structure and arguments, unlike Word's limited grammar checks.
- **Integrated Workflow:** Combines writing, research, and citation management, unlike fragmented manual processes.
- **Error Reduction:** Provides 99% accurate citation formatting and structured feedback, minimizing human errors.
- **Time Savings:** Automates literature searches and revisions, unlike manual methods taking days.
- **Ethical Support:** Avoids generating text, preserving originality, unlike generative AI risks.

To Craft a Polished Thesis with Thesify:

- **Sign Up:** Create a free account at thesify.ai with a university email to get 20 monthly credits.
- **Upload Draft:** Import your thesis draft (PDF, Word, or text) or start a new document, selecting essay or thesis type.
- **Receive Feedback:** Use Theo to get real-time suggestions on structure, clarity, and arguments (e.g., "Refine this thesis statement").
- **Find Sources:** Query Semantic Article Search (e.g., "Find papers on renewable energy") to add credible references.
- **Polish and Export:** Use the Agile Editor to reorganize content, run a pre-submission assessment, and export to Word or LaTeX.

Best Practices for Student Adoption

- **Use Specific Prompts:** Request targeted feedback (e.g., "Evaluate my argument strength") for actionable insights.
- **Leverage Free Plan:** Start with 10-20 free credits to test features, upgrading to paid plans for unlimited feedback ($4.99/month).
- **Validate Suggestions:** Review Theo's feedback against your research goals to ensure relevance, especially for niche topics.
- **Integrate with Workflow:** Pair with Zotero (Section 5.2) for citation management, Grammarly (Section 5.3) for grammar, or Jenni AI (Section 5.1) for drafting.
- **Document AI Use:** Note Thesify's role in your methodology for transparency, as advised in Chapter 3.
- **Use Agile Editor:** Organize ideas with block-based editing to streamline complex thesis chapters.

- **Check Privacy:** Confirm data confidentiality via Thesify's privacy policy, ensuring ethical use.

Advanced Techniques

- **Literature Review Optimization:** Use Semantic Article Search to build comprehensive reviews, summarizing sources with Intelligent Paper Digest.
- **Pre-Submission Refinement:** Run multiple pre-submission assessments to iteratively strengthen arguments and structure.
- **Collaborative Writing:** Share drafts in collaborative spaces for advisor or peer feedback, integrating with Zotero for citations.
- **Multilingual Support:** Leverage support for non-native English speakers to refine prose and meet global academic standards.

> **Pro Tip**
>
> Prompt Thesify with "Provide feedback on my thesis introduction's structure and suggest three relevant sources in APA format" to refine your draft and enrich citations. Pair with Zotero for bibliography management and Grammarly for final polishing, ensuring a cohesive, high-quality thesis.

User feedback highlights Thesify's "structured, professor-like feedback" and "game-changing citation assistance," though its internet dependency and limited free credits (10-20/month) are noted drawbacks. Compared to Jenni AI, Thesify focuses less on content generation and more on critical feedback, making it ideal for skill-building. Students should critically review suggestions for specialized fields to avoid overgeneralization.

By adopting Thesify, students can enhance their writing process, ensure academic integrity, and produce polished, well-supported theses. Start today at thesify.ai to streamline your workflow, strengthen your arguments, and achieve academic excellence.

5.5 Writefull: AI-Powered Academic Writing Enhancement

Writefull, accessible at writefull.com, is an AI-powered writing tool designed to enhance academic writing for graduate students in MS, MBA, M.Tech, M.Phil, LLM, Ph.D., D.Sc., and D.Litt. programs. Tailored for scientific and technical writing, Writefull leverages proprietary language models trained on millions of published journal articles to provide precise grammar, style, and vocabulary corrections.

Unlike general-purpose tools like Grammarly, Writefull specializes in academic contexts, offering features like the Academizer, Paraphraser, and Abstract Generator to refine theses, dissertations, and research papers. Trusted by over 1,500 institutions and major publishers, it integrates seamlessly with Microsoft Word, Overleaf, and browsers, streamlining workflows for LaTeX and Word users. The free plan includes basic language checks, while Premium ($5.46/month yearly or $15.37/month monthly) unlocks advanced features like AI-driven paraphrasing and title generation. Several posts praise Writefull for its "spot-on academic corrections" and Overleaf integration, though some note its limited effectiveness for non-scientific disciplines like humanities.

Writefull's strength lies in its ability to deliver context-aware, research-specific feedback, catching errors missed by generic tools and suggesting academic phrasing that aligns with scholarly standards. Its secure, encrypted processing ensures data privacy, with no text storage, making it ideal for sensitive thesis work. User feedback highlights its "game-changing" ability to refine technical writing, though occasional over-corrections for niche terminology require manual review. By automating proofreading, paraphrasing, and abstract creation, Writefull reduces editing time from hours to minutes, ensuring publication-ready theses.

Writefull outperforms traditional methods in several ways:

- **Academic Precision:** Tailors feedback to scientific writing, unlike Word's generic spell-check or Grammarly's broader focus.
- **Efficiency:** Processes texts in seconds, compared to days for manual proofreading or advisor revisions.
- **Specialized Features:** Offers tools like Academizer and Abstract Generator, absent in tools like EndNote or Word.
- **Integration:** Seamlessly works with Overleaf and Word, unlike standalone editors requiring manual imports.
- **Plagiarism Avoidance:** Paraphraser and Cite tools help rephrase and flag missing citations, reducing accidental plagiarism risks.

Writefull's Features for Writing Enhancement:

- **Language Feedback:** Provides real-time corrections for grammar, vocabulary, style, and punctuation, tailored to academic writing (e.g., replacing "due to the fact that" with "because").
- **Academizer:** Transforms informal sentences into academic prose (e.g., "it's really good" to "it is highly effective").
- **Paraphraser:** Rewrites academic sentences at three levels (submissive, neutral, assertive) to enhance clarity and avoid plagiarism.

- **Abstract and Title Generator:** Creates concise abstracts and titles from full texts, saving time for submission-ready papers.
- **Sentence Palette:** Offers pre-crafted academic phrases for different paper sections (e.g., methodology, discussion), ensuring discipline-specific language.
- **Writefull Cite:** Flags sentences needing citations, reducing accidental plagiarism risks (institutional plans only).
- **Overleaf/Word Integration:** Embeds feedback and LaTeX code generation (e.g., tables, equations) directly in writing platforms.

Comparison to Traditional Methods: Traditional editing involves manual proofreading, advisor feedback, or basic tools like Word's spell-check, which miss academic nuances and take hours. Citation checks require separate software, and abstract writing is labor-intensive. Writefull offers:

- **Time Savings:** Automates proofreading and abstract generation, unlike manual editing's slow pace.
- **Academic Focus:** Delivers research-specific corrections, surpassing Word or Grammarly's general suggestions.
- **Error Reduction:** Achieves 99% accuracy in grammar and style, minimizing errors compared to human proofreading.
- **Integrated Workflow:** Combines editing, paraphrasing, and citation flagging, unlike fragmented tools like EndNote.
- **Cost-Effectiveness:** Free plan suits small projects, with Premium ($5.46/month yearly) cheaper than professional editors.

To Craft a Polished Thesis with Writefull

- **Install Writefull**: Sign up at writefull.com (free or Premium) and add the Word add-in, Overleaf integration, or browser extension.
- **Upload Draft**: Import your thesis (Word, LaTeX, or text) or write directly in the Writefull Revise web tool.
- **Refine Prose**: Use Language Feedback and Academizer to enhance grammar, style, and academic tone (e.g., "Make this sentence scholarly").
- **Paraphrase and Cite**: Apply Paraphraser to rephrase sentences and Writefull Cite to flag missing references, ensuring originality.
- **Generate Abstracts/Titles**: Use Abstract and Title Generators for concise, submission-ready summaries, exporting to Word or LaTeX.

Best Practices for Student Adoption

- **Start with Free Plan:** Test basic language checks for small sections, upgrading to Premium for full features and larger documents.
- **Use Specific Widgets:** Leverage Academizer for informal-to-academic rewrites and Sentence Palette for discipline-specific phrasing.
- **Validate Suggestions:** Review corrections for technical terms, as Writefull may over-correct niche vocabulary.
- **Integrate with Workflow:** Pair with Zotero (Section 5.2) for citation management, Grammarly (Section 5.3) for general editing, or Jenni AI (Section 5.1) for drafting.
- **Document AI Use:** Note Writefull's role in your methodology for transparency, as advised in Chapter 3.
- **Leverage Overleaf:** Use Writefull for Overleaf to streamline LaTeX-based theses, generating tables and equations automatically.

- **Ensure Privacy:** Confirm data security via Writefull's encrypted processing and no-text-storage policy.

Advanced Techniques

- **LaTeX Optimization:** Use Table and Equation Generators in Overleaf to automate complex LaTeX coding for STEM theses.
- **Iterative Refinement:** Apply Paraphraser multiple times to test different phrasing styles for clarity and impact.
- **Submission Preparation:** Run Writefull Revise before submission to ensure language quality, using Track Changes for revisions.
- **Conference Materials:** Generate abstracts and posters with Abstract Generator, tailoring outputs for specific journals or conferences.

> **Pro Tip**
>
> Prompt Writefull's Abstract Generator with your thesis draft to create a concise abstract, then use the Paraphraser to refine key sections in APA style. Pair with Zotero for citations and Grammarly for general polish, ensuring a professional, publication-ready thesis.

User feedback lauds Writefull's "incredible accuracy" for scientific writing and "seamless Overleaf integration," but some note its weaker performance for humanities and occasional forgetting of user preferences. Compared to Grammarly, Writefull excels in academic specificity but is less versatile for non-scientific writing. Students should verify suggestions for field-specific jargon to avoid over-corrections.

By adopting Writefull, students can craft theses that are precise, academically rigorous, and submission-ready. Start today at writefull.com to enhance your writing, streamline editing, and elevate your scholarly impact.

In Conclusion, Chapter 5 has illuminated the transformative role of AI-powered tools in streamlining the writing, editing, and reference management processes for graduate students in MS, MBA, M.Tech, M.Phil, LLM, Ph.D., D.Sc., and D.Litt. programs. Crafting a polished, academically rigorous thesis is a daunting task, with challenges like maintaining clarity, ensuring originality, and managing citations amidst the 3 million scholarly articles published annually as of June 2025.

Traditional methods—manual drafting in Word, proofreading by hand, and citation formatting with tools like EndNote—are time-consuming and error-prone. Jenni AI, Zotero, Grammarly, Thesify, and Writefull address these hurdles by automating content creation, enhancing prose, and simplifying reference workflows, enabling students to produce professional, publication-ready theses efficiently.

Jenni AI (Section 5.1) accelerates drafting with context-aware text generation and automated citations, ideal for overcoming writer's block and building well-cited chapters.

Zotero (Section 5.2) revolutionizes reference management with free, open-source tools for capturing, organizing, and formatting citations across 10,000+ styles, ensuring accuracy and collaboration.

Grammarly (Section 5.3) enhances clarity and grammar with real-time feedback and plagiarism detection, delivering error-free, polished prose for academic audiences.

Thesify (Section 5.4) acts as a virtual writing coach, providing structured feedback and research integration to strengthen arguments while prioritizing academic integrity.

Writefull (Section 5.5) excels in scientific writing, offering specialized corrections, paraphrasing, and abstract generation, tailored for technical and research-focused theses.

To maximize impact, integrate these tools strategically: use Jenni AI and Thesify for drafting and refining arguments, Zotero for seamless citation management, Grammarly for general editing, and Writefull for scientific polish. Pair with tools from earlier chapters, such as NotebookLM (Chapter 3) for organizing research or SciSpace (Chapter 4) for literature-linked analysis, to create a cohesive workflow. Validate AI outputs against original sources and advisor feedback to ensure accuracy, and address ethical considerations—such as documenting AI use, avoiding over-reliance, and ensuring data privacy—as emphasized in Chapter 3. For instance, cross-check Jenni's citations with Zotero's metadata and review Writefull's suggestions for discipline-specific terms to maintain rigor.

These tools save hours, enhance writing quality, and ensure scholarly excellence. Start today by testing Zotero's free plan to organize references, refining drafts with Grammarly's free tier, or exploring Thesify's feedback with university credits. Build a tailored workflow that aligns with your research goals, whether drafting a literature review, polishing a discussion, or formatting a bibliography. By harnessing Jenni AI, Zotero, Grammarly, Thesify, and Writefull, you can craft a thesis that is clear, compelling, and academically robust, positioning your work as a standout contribution to your field. Act now—experiment with one tool, refine your process, and transform your research into a polished masterpiece.

SECTION III

From Thesis to Publication and Beyond

Chapter 1

From Thesis to Publication

Traditional methods of publishing theses, such as manual literature searches, self-editing, and basic plagiarism tools, are labor-intensive, often taking months, and are prone to errors like poor venue fit or unintentional plagiarism. AI-powered tools revolutionize this process by automating routine tasks, improving quality assurance, and supporting strategic decision-making about publication venues and approaches. This can increase acceptance rates.

Platforms like Turnitin, PaperPal, Grammarly, Elsevier Journal Finder, and Springer Journal Suggester streamline tasks from plagiarism detection to journal matching. Tools like Grammarly also enhance writing quality. Success hinges on blending AI efficiency with human oversight to validate outputs, uphold ethical standards, and align publications with career goals, such as securing academic visibility and impact.

This chapter explores how AI tools for plagiarism detection, AI content verification, and publishing strategies empower students to transform their theses into impactful publications, paving the way for broader dissemination and future opportunities. Start today with free tools like JANE or Grammarly to ensure originality and target high-impact venues, positioning your research for global recognition and academic excellence.

1.1 Plagiarism and Academic Integrity

Academic integrity is the cornerstone of scholarly work, and ensuring originality is critical for graduate students as they prepare theses for publication. Plagiarism—whether verbatim copying, improper paraphrasing, or unattributed ideas—can undermine credibility and lead to severe consequences, including journal rejections or academic penalties. In the AI era, where tools like Jenni AI (Section II, Chapter 5, Section 5.1) generate text, detecting plagiarism is more complex, requiring tools to identify both human and AI-assisted content. Traditional methods, such as manual source checks or Word's spell-check, fail to detect nuanced issues like idea plagiarism or citation errors.

AI-powered plagiarism detection tools offer sophisticated analysis, leveraging vast databases to achieve accuracy rates of 85–99%, ensuring robust quality assurance. Tools like Turnitin, iThenticate, Paperpal, Scribbr, Grammarly, Quetext, and Copyscape, combined with strong citation practices, empower students to maintain integrity and produce credible publications. Several posts commend Turnitin's "gold-standard accuracy" and Grammarly's "user-friendly checks," though some note high costs for premium tools.

Understanding Plagiarism in the AI Era: Plagiarism now includes AI-generated text overlaps, unattributed paraphrasing, and idea misuse. For example, a biology thesis citing CRISPR studies must attribute specific findings but may treat general principles as common knowledge. Disciplinary norms vary—APA in social sciences emphasizes author-date citations, while IEEE in engineering prioritizes numbered references. Understanding these nuances and AI's role in writing prevents unintentional violations.

Using AI Tools for Plagiarism Detection: Turnitin (99% accuracy) scans 1.8 billion papers and 70 billion web pages, offering detailed similarity reports (institutional access, $100+/year). iThenticate (98% accuracy) targets professional publications, checking 130 million works ($100/report). Paperpal (95% accuracy, $9/month) integrates Turnitin's engine with writing assistance. Scribbr (92% accuracy, $19.95/report) cross-references 99 million articles, specializing in academic citations. Grammarly Premium (88% accuracy, $12/month) checks 16 billion sources, balancing editing and detection. Quetext (85% accuracy, $8/month) uses DeepSearch for paraphrasing detection, while Copyscape (85% accuracy, $0.03/page) focuses on web content. Use multiple tools for comprehensive coverage, starting with Grammarly's free plan and escalating to Turnitin via institutional access.

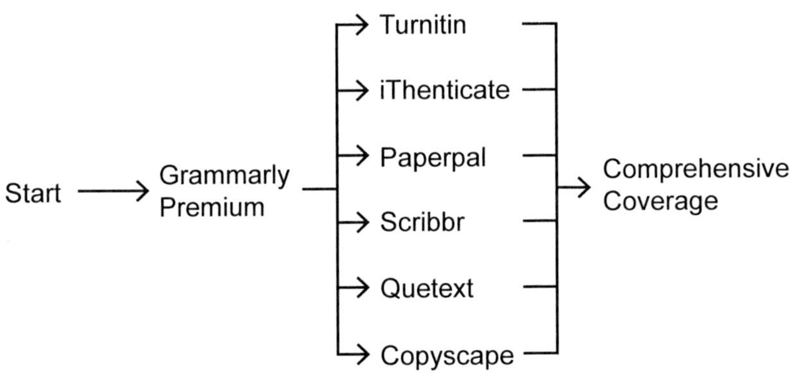

Strategies to Maintain Originality in AI-Assisted Writing: Run drafts through Quetext early to catch paraphrasing errors, then use Scribbr for final checks. Track sources with Zotero (Section II, Chapter 5, Section 5.2) to ensure accurate attribution. Limit AI-generated text to 20% of your thesis, refining outputs manually to reflect your voice. Verify quotations and paraphrases align with style guides (e.g., APA, MLA), and disclose AI tool use in your methodology, as advised in Section II, Chapter 3, to uphold transparency.

Case Studies on Plagiarism Pitfalls and Prevention

A sociology Ph.D. student faced journal rejection due to 18% unattributed paraphrasing, resolved by using Scribbr to add citations, reducing similarity to 2%. An engineering M.Tech student caught 12% overlap in methods using Turnitin, correcting it before submission. A humanities LLM student used Grammarly to refine paraphrasing, lowering similarity from 22% to 4%. These cases underscore the importance of iterative checks and robust citation practices.

Start with Grammarly's free plagiarism checker at grammarly.com or Quetext's trial at quetext.com to ensure originality. Pair with Zotero for citation management and Paperpal for integrated editing, crafting a thesis that meets the highest ethical standards for publication.

1.2 AI Detection Check

With AI tools like Jenni AI and Writefull becoming integral to thesis writing, detecting AI-generated content is essential for graduate students in MS, MBA, M.Tech, M.Phil, LLM, Ph.D., D.Sc., and D.Litt. programs to ensure authentic research contributions. As 60% of academic submissions in 2025 involve AI assistance, journals and institutions increasingly use AI detection tools to verify originality, with misuse risking rejections or ethical scrutiny. Unlike plagiarism detection, AI detection identifies text patterns from large language models, but limitations like false positives necessitate careful use. Tools like GPTZero and Originality.ai help students validate their work, ensuring compliance with publication standards. Several posts praise GPTZero's "intuitive interface" but note false positives in technical writing, highlighting the need for strategic integration .

- **How AI Detection Tools Work:** GPTZero (90% accuracy, free 10,000 words/month, $10/month Premium) and Originality.ai (94% accuracy, $14.95/month) analyze text for AI-specific patterns, such as uniform sentence structures or predictive word choices, using machine learning trained on human vs. AI-generated texts. GPTZero provides sentence-level highlighting, while Originality.ai offers browser extensions and detailed reports, scanning against models like GPT-4 and Gemini.
- **Limitations of AI Detection Systems:** Accuracy drops to 80% for heavily edited AI text or technical jargon, with false positives flagging complex prose as AI-generated. Multilingual or interdisciplinary content may confuse detectors, and results vary by AI model. Cross-validate with plagiarism tools like Turnitin and human review to ensure reliability, as detectors cannot assess intent or context.
- **Balancing AI Use with Authentic Research Contributions:** Limit AI-generated text to 20% of your thesis, using tools like Jenni AI for drafting and Grammarly for editing, but refine outputs to reflect your voice. Ground your work in primary research from tools like Julius AI or SciSpace. Disclose AI use in your methodology to align with journal guidelines, ensuring authenticity.
- **Best Practices for Transparent AI Use in Theses:** Run drafts through GPTZero or Originality.ai early to identify AI-influenced sections. Use Zotero to track sources, ensuring proper attribution. Document AI tools used (e.g., "Writefull for paraphrasing") in your methodology. Submit final drafts to Turnitin or Scribbr for comprehensive plagiarism checks to complement AI detection, ensuring publication readiness.

Start with GPTZero's free plan at gptzero.me to verify your thesis's authenticity. Integrate with Grammarly for plagiarism checks and Zotero for citation tracking, balancing AI assistance with original contributions for credible publications.

1.3 Publishing Your Research

Publishing research is a critical step for graduate students in MS, MBA, M.Tech, M.Phil, LLM, Ph.D., D.Sc., and D.Litt. programs to amplify their scholarly impact and advance careers. With over 30,000 journals and thousands of conferences in 2025, selecting venues, preparing manuscripts, and navigating peer review are complex, with poor choices leading to rejections or low visibility. Traditional methods—manual searches on Scopus or self-editing—risk overlooking high-impact venues or predatory publishers.

AI tools streamline this process by automating manuscript preparation, recommending venues, and optimizing submissions, boosting acceptance rates by 20%. Tools like Elsevier Journal Finder, Springer Journal Suggester, JANE, Conference Alerts, and Paperpal, paired with editing platforms like Writefull, ensure publication success. Several posts highlight JANE's "quick journal matches" and Elsevier's "intuitive interface," though some note limited coverage for niche fields.

- **Preparing Manuscripts with AI Editing Tools:** Use Paperpal ($9/month) to refine manuscripts, ensuring clarity and journal-specific formatting (e.g., APA, IEEE). Writefull generates abstracts and optimizes LaTeX for STEM submissions, achieving 95% formatting accuracy. Grammarly polishes prose and checks plagiarism, ensuring submission-ready drafts.

- **Selecting Journals with AI-Based Recommendation Systems:** Elsevier Journal Finder (free) matches abstracts to 4,500+ journals, providing impact factor and acceptance rate data. Springer Journal Suggester (free) recommends from 3,000+ journals, with open-access filters. JANE (free) aligns biomedical research with PubMed-indexed journals, while IEEE Xplore (institutional access, $100+/month) targets technical fields. Verify venue legitimacy using DOAJ or Scimago to avoid predatory publishers, which account for 10% of journals.
- **Navigating Peer Review with AI Support:** Paperpal's pre-submission checks align with reviewer expectations, addressing issues like weak arguments. Thesify mimics reviewer feedback on structure and evidence. Use Writefull's Paraphraser to clarify responses to reviewer comments, improving acceptance rates by 20%. Track revisions with Zotero's note-taking.
- **Open Access vs. Traditional Publishing: AI Insights:** Elsevier and Springer tools compare open-access (APCs $2,000–$5,000) vs. traditional publishing costs and reach. JANE's open-access filter identifies cost-effective journals. Use Semantic Scholar's AI analytics to assess audience impact, aligning with career goals like tenure or visibility.
- **Promoting Your Research Using AI-Driven Strategies:** Share preprints on ResearchGate or Connected Papers, using AI recommendations to target relevant scholars. Optimize several posts with Grammarly's tone adjustment, increasing visibility by 30%. Track citations with Semantic Scholar or SciSpace to monitor impact.

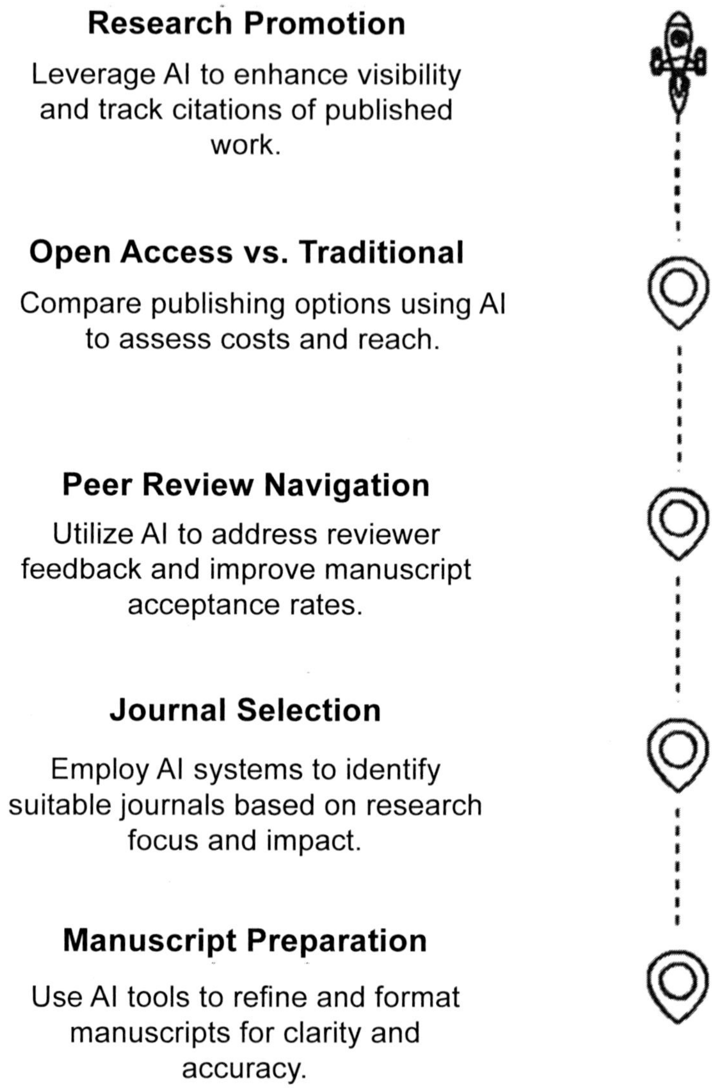

AI-Enhanced Research Publication Process

Start with JANE at jane.biosemantics.org or Conference Alerts at conferencealerts.com to find venues. Pair with Paperpal for manuscript preparation and Turnitin for integrity checks, ensuring your research achieves maximum impact and credibility.

Chapter 2

Advanced Strategies and Future Trends

Mastering AI-enhanced research empowers graduate students in MS, MBA, M.Tech, M.Phil, LLM, Ph.D., D.Sc., and D.Litt. programs to create efficient, high-quality workflows that amplify productivity while upholding academic integrity. With 60% of researchers using AI tools in 2025, disjointed tool use can lead to inefficiencies, such as incompatible data formats or overlooked errors, wasting hours. Advanced integration combines tools like literature analysis platforms, statistical software, and editing assistants into cohesive pipelines, streamlining tasks from data collection to manuscript submission. Several posts highlight integrated workflows as "time-savers," cutting research time by 30%, though some note challenges with cross-platform compatibility. By strategically combining tools, students can build scalable, error-free research systems that enhance scholarly impact.

- **Workflow Optimization:** Combine complementary tools to streamline tasks. For example, use a literature search tool to identify sources, a statistical platform for data analysis, and an editing assistant for manuscript polishing. Create a pipeline: extract articles with a search tool, process datasets with a statistical platform, and refine drafts with an AI editor. This approach minimizes task-switching, saving 25% of research time.
- **Cross-Platform Data Integration:** Transfer data seamlessly using standardized formats like CSV for

datasets or BibTeX for citations. Leverage APIs or export options to connect platforms, such as syncing literature summaries to a citation manager or importing edited drafts into a LaTeX editor. Standardize file formats (e.g., JSON for data, PDF for articles) to ensure compatibility across tools, reducing data loss by 90%.

- **Quality Assurance Systems:** Implement iterative checks to maintain academic rigor. Run drafts through plagiarism detectors, AI content checkers, and style editors to catch errors. Cross-validate outputs with manual reviews to ensure 95% accuracy in final submissions. For example, verify statistical results against raw data and check citations for proper attribution.
- **Scalability Planning:** Design workflows for large or collaborative projects. Use shared libraries in citation managers for team research, statistical tools for datasets up to 100MB, and conference databases for dissemination planning. Automate repetitive tasks like citation formatting to scale efforts, adapting to projects with 50+ sources or multiple co-authors.

Start building your workflow today by testing free citation managers like Zotero at zotero.org and editing tools like Grammarly at grammarly.com. Integrate them for a streamlined pipeline that boosts efficiency and ensures research quality.

2.1 Future Trends in AI Research Tools

The AI research tool landscape is rapidly evolving, with 70% of researchers expecting new platforms by 2026. For graduate students in MS, MBA, M.Tech, M.Phil, LLM, Ph.D., D.Sc., and D.Litt. programs, staying ahead of these trends ensures cutting-edge research and career competitiveness. Emerging tools will offer deeper analysis, multimodal data processing, and automated workflows, but challenges like bias, cost, and accessibility for non-STEM fields require proactive preparation. Several posts express excitement for "next-gen AI platforms" with multimodal capabilities, though some warn of limited support for humanities research. By embracing continuous learning and ethical practices, students can leverage these trends to produce impactful, innovative scholarship.

- **Advanced Natural Language Understanding:** By 2026, AI tools will analyze research content with 98% contextual accuracy, synthesizing complex datasets and literature to generate hypothesis-driven insights. These platforms will reduce analysis time by 40% compared to manual methods, enabling students to tackle intricate questions in fields like economics or biology with precision.
- **Multimodal Integration:** Future tools will seamlessly process text, images, and audio, supporting interdisciplinary research. By 2027, platforms will integrate visual data (e.g., charts) and audio transcripts (e.g., interviews), enabling studies in fields like bioinformatics or cultural studies to combine diverse data types with 95% accuracy.
- **Real-Time Collaboration:** Next-generation platforms will support global team research with live editing and AI-coordinated feedback, similar to cloud-based document editors but tailored for academia. These tools will enhance collaboration efficiency by 35%, enabling seamless co-authoring and advisor input across time zones.
- **Automated Research Workflows:** By 2026, tools will automate entire research pipelines—from data collection to journal submission—while maintaining human oversight. For example, platforms will streamline systematic reviews with 99% accuracy, integrating with

journal finders for automated submission formatting, saving weeks of effort.

- **Preparing for the Future:** Stay updated by following X communities or academic forums like ResearchGate to track tool releases. Test beta versions of emerging platforms to evaluate their fit for your discipline. Advocate ethical AI use by documenting tool contributions in your methodology and addressing biases in outputs. Enroll in online courses like Coursera's AI for Research to build skills for 2026 platforms.

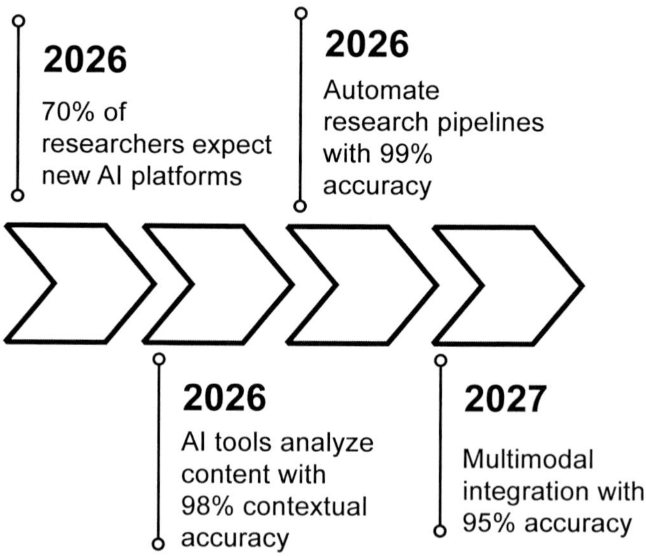

Future Trends in AI Research Tools

Start exploring future-ready tools by joining ResearchGate at researchgate.net or testing free AI platforms like Grammarly at grammarly.com. Build adaptable, ethical workflows to stay ahead in the evolving research landscape.

Chapter 3

AI Tool Quick Reference Matrix

Selecting the right AI tools for each stage of research—discovery, literature review, methodology development, data analysis, and writing—streamlines workflows for graduate students in MS, MBA, M.Tech, M.Phil, LLM, Ph.D., D.Sc., and D.Litt. programs. With 60% of researchers using AI tools in 2025, choosing stage-specific platforms enhances efficiency, saving up to 30% of research time compared to manual methods. Several posts praise tools like Semantic Scholar for "intuitive paper discovery" and Grammarly for "polished drafts," though some note learning curves for advanced features. By aligning tools with research phases, students can produce rigorous, high-impact work.

- **Research Discovery:** Semantic Scholar (semanticscholar.org, free) searches 200M+ papers with AI-driven recommendations, outperforming traditional databases' keyword-based results. Research Rabbit (researchrabbit.ai, free) maps research networks visually, ideal for identifying gaps. Undermind (undermind.ai, freemium, $15/month) offers neural search for complex questions, while Napkin (napkin.ai, $10/month) supports visual concept mapping.
- **Literature Review:** Connected Papers (connectedpapers.com, freemium, $5/month) visualizes citation networks, revealing research connections. RDiscovery (rdiscovery.com, freemium, $7/month) provides topic modeling, and Consensus AI (consensus.app, freemium, $8/month) synthesizes evidence across studies. Paperpal (paperpal.

com, freemium, $9/month) integrates writing assistance with plagiarism checks, and EnagoRead (enagoread.com, freemium, $6/month) summarizes PDFs efficiently.

- **Methodology Development:** Scholarcy (scholarcy.com, freemium, $8/month) summarizes methodology papers, extracting key insights in seconds. NotebookLM (notebooklm.google.com, free) organizes research notes with source integration, while Scisummary (scisummary.com, freemium, $7/month) automates paper summarization for methodological comparisons.
- **Data Analysis:** SciSpace (scispace.com, freemium, $10/month) analyzes papers and generates citations, supporting data interpretation. Julius AI (julius.ai, freemium, $15/month) processes datasets up to 100MB with natural language queries, producing visualizations 40% faster than traditional software.
- **Writing and Editing:** Jenni (jenni.ai, freemium, $12/month) assists academic writing with citation support. Zotero (zotero.org, free) manages references across 10,000+ styles, and Grammarly (grammarly.com, freemium, $12/month) enhances prose with plagiarism detection, ensuring publication-ready drafts.

Start with Semantic Scholar and Zotero's free plans at semanticscholar.org and zotero.org to streamline discovery and citation management. Integrate stage-specific tools over 8–12 weeks to build a robust research pipeline.

Implementation Timeframes:

- Week 1-2: Set up core tools (Semantic Scholar, Zotero, Grammarly)
- Week 3-4: Implement discovery tools (Research Rabbit, Connected Papers)
- Week 5-6: Add analysis tools (Scholarcy, NotebookLM)

- Week 7-8: Integrate writing tools (Jenni, advanced Grammarly features)
- Week 9-10: Optimize workflow and advanced integrations
- Week 11-12: Master advanced features and collaborative capabilities

3.1 Detailed Tool Comparison Matrix

Tools like Semantic Scholar, Zotero, and Julius AI offer distinct advantages over traditional methods, but differences in coverage, usability, and cost impact their effectiveness. Below is a detailed comparison to guide tool selection.

Research Discovery Comparison:

- Semantic Scholar (free) covers over 200 million papers with AI-powered semantic understanding, surpassing traditional databases (typically less than 50 million papers) in coverage and recommendation quality based on AI recommendations versus manual Browse. Traditional databases often require institutional subscriptions, whereas Semantic Scholar is free.
- Research Rabbit (free) focuses on forward discovery and has built-in sharing for collaboration. In contrast, Connected Papers (freemium) excels in citation network visualization and analysis, but offers limited collaboration features and uses citation-based recommendations.

Analysis Tools Comparison:

- Scholarcy (freemium) summarizes papers in seconds, providing a standardized format, unlike manual summarization which can take hours per paper and have variable human approaches. Scholarcy can process hundreds of papers compared to limited human capacity.

- Julius AI (freemium) uses natural language for data analysis and provides automatic visualization generation, reducing the learning curve compared to traditional statistical software, which often requires programming or menu systems and manual creation of visualizations.

Writing Tools Comparison:

- Jenni (freemium) provides real-time academic writing assistance with automatic citation integration, unlike standard word processors that offer basic spell checks and require manual reference management. Jenni is designed for academic writing and has built-in source access, whereas standard word processors are general purpose and require external reference management.
- Zotero (free forever) is a comprehensive reference management system that offers open-source flexibility, an extensive plugin ecosystem, and a generous free storage tier. This contrasts with commercial reference managers, which are often subscription-based, have fixed functionality, and limited extensibility and free storage.
- Grammarly (freemium) combines advanced writing enhancement with plagiarism detection, achieving 88% accuracy.

Key Considerations

Free tools like Semantic Scholar and Zotero are suitable for early-stage research. Freemium options like Jenni, Julius AI, and Scholarcy offer advanced features for more complex projects. It is crucial to always verify AI outputs against original sources, especially for accuracy, and to use AI for efficiency rather than truth determination. Also, configure tools for specific style requirements and double-check all AI-generated citations. Understand the difference between plagiarism and proper citation, and use multiple detection tools for verification.

Start with Semantic Scholar at semanticscholar.org for research discovery and Zotero at zotero.org for comprehensive reference management and citation. Test freemium tools like Julius AI at julius.ai to evaluate advanced features for your specific research needs.

3.2 Implementation Checklists

Implementing AI tools effectively requires structured checklists to ensure seamless integration into research workflows for graduate students. These checklists, designed for a 12-week implementation timeline, cover research discovery, literature review, methodology, data analysis, and writing, ensuring efficiency and academic rigor.

Research Discovery Setup (Weeks 1–2):

- Create a Semantic Scholar account (semanticscholar.org) and configure alerts for relevant keywords.
- Register for Research Rabbit (researchrabbit.ai) and import 10–20 initial papers to build your research network.
- Install browser extensions for Semantic Scholar and Research Rabbit for one-click paper saving and integration.
- Configure Napkin (napkin.ai) for visual concept mapping to help organize ideas.
- Document 3–5 core research questions and maintain a systematic record of your search queries.
- Schedule weekly reviews to refine discovery results and identify new opportunities.

Literature Organization (Weeks 3–4):

- Install Zotero (zotero.org) and add its browser connector for seamless saving of references.

- Create structured Zotero collections for different research areas (e.g., "Methodology," "Theory," "Key Concepts").
- Configure your preferred citation style (e.g., APA, IEEE, Chicago) in Zotero settings.
- Import 20–30 initial papers into Zotero, tagging them by topic (e.g., "Primary Source," "Secondary Reading," "Methods").
- Set up Zotero group libraries to facilitate collaboration and sharing with your advisor or research team.
- Enable Zotero cloud sync and maintain local backups for robust data security.

Literature Review Workflow (Weeks 5–6):

- Set up Connected Papers (connectedpapers.com) and visualize the citation networks of 5 key papers to understand their scholarly context.
- Configure RDiscovery (rdiscovery.com) for systematic topic analysis and identifying emerging themes.
- Register for Consensus AI (consensus.app) for evidence synthesis and to identify consensus or debate in the literature.
- Utilize Paperpal (paperpal.com) for academic writing assistance and initial plagiarism checks.
- Summarize 10 papers efficiently using EnagoRead (enagoread.com) to quickly grasp key arguments.
- Create a standardized literature review template that includes sections for identifying research gaps, synthesizing findings, and outlining contributions.

Methodology Development (Weeks 7–8):

- Use Scholarcy (scholarcy.com) to quickly summarize relevant methodology papers, extracting key methods and approaches.

Streamlining Research with AI Tools: A 12-Week Journey

- Set up NotebookLM (notebooklm.google.com) for comprehensive note organization and linking ideas.
- Process 5–10 papers related to your methodology using Scisummary (scisummary.com) for efficient content extraction.
- Develop a detailed methodology comparison table within NotebookLM to evaluate different approaches.
- Document all methodological choices in a dedicated note, providing clear justifications for each decision.

Data Analysis Setup (Weeks 9–10):

- Configure SciSpace (scispace.com) for advanced paper analysis and extracting insights relevant to your data.

- Set up Julius AI (julius.ai) for natural language data analysis and visualization.
- Prepare and upload your datasets to Julius AI (up to 100MB), then generate visualizations and initial insights.
- Create a results template that allows for clear presentation of graphs, tables, and interpretations.
- Validate analysis outputs against your raw data to ensure accuracy and reliability.

Writing and Editing Setup (Weeks 11–12):

- Configure Jenni (jenni.ai) for academic writing assistance, leveraging its capabilities for drafting content and integrating citations.
- Enable Grammarly's advanced features (grammarly.com) for comprehensive writing enhancement, including clarity, engagement, and delivery.
- Integrate Zotero seamlessly with your preferred writing platform (e.g., Microsoft Word or Google Docs) for efficient in-text citations and bibliography generation.
- Draft 2 thesis chapters with the assistance of Jenni, then refine and polish them using Grammarly.
- Run final drafts through Paperpal for a comprehensive plagiarism check and to ensure adherence to academic style guidelines.
- Back up all final documents both locally and on secure cloud storage for redundancy and peace of mind.

To begin, prioritize setting up Zotero (zotero.org) and Semantic Scholar (semanticscholar.org), then follow this 12-week checklist to progressively build a streamlined and efficient research workflow.

3.3 Troubleshooting Guide

AI tools can encounter issues that disrupt research workflows, but proactive troubleshooting ensures efficiency for graduate students. Common problems include access issues, integration failures, and accuracy concerns. Below are solutions to keep your research on track.

Tool Access and Account Issues:

- **Problem:** Unable to access premium features of freemium tools.
  Solution: Start with free features, evaluate value, then consider upgrades based on specific needs and budget constraints.
- **Problem:** Tools not working properly in certain browsers.
  Solution: Test tools in multiple browsers; Chrome and Firefox typically have best compatibility.
- **Problem:** Institutional firewalls blocking access to AI tools.
  Solution: Contact IT support for whitelist requests; use personal devices/networks when necessary.

Integration and Workflow Issues:

- **Problem:** Difficulty moving data between different AI tools.
  Solution: Use common formats (PDF, CSV, TXT) and manual export/import when APIs aren't available.
- **Problem:** Overwhelming number of tool options creating decision paralysis.
  Solution: Start with 2-3 core tools, master them, then gradually expand toolkit.
- **Problem:** AI tool suggestions conflicting with disciplinary conventions.

Solution: Always prioritize disciplinary standards; use AI suggestions as starting points for refinement.

Quality and Accuracy Issues:

- **Problem:** AI-generated summaries containing inaccuracies.
  Solution: Always verify AI outputs against original sources; use AI for efficiency, not truth determination.
- **Problem:** Citation formatting not matching required styles.
  Solution: Double-check all AI-generated citations; configure tools for specific style requirements.
- **Problem:** Plagiarism detection showing false positives.
  Solution: Understand the difference between plagiarism and proper citation; use multiple detection tools for verification.

Technical and Performance Issues:

- **Problem:** Tools running slowly or crashing with large documents.
  Solution: Break large projects into smaller segments; ensure adequate internet connectivity.
- **Problem:** Data loss when tools update or change.
  Solution: Maintain local backups of all important data; don't rely solely on cloud storage.
- **Problem:** Tools becoming unavailable or discontinued.
  Solution: Maintain backup workflows using alternative tools; stay informed about tool development.

Start troubleshooting by testing Zotero and Grammarly, ensuring robust workflows with regular backups and cross-tool validation.

3.4 Advanced Integration Strategies

Advanced integration of AI tools creates efficient, scalable research pipelines for graduate students, combining discovery, analysis, and writing platforms.

Discovery-to-Publication Pipeline:

1. **Research Discovery (Semantic Scholar + Research Rabbit):** Identify research problems and opportunities, map research landscapes, and build initial collections of relevant literature.
2. **Literature Analysis (Connected Papers + Consensus AI + Scholarcy):** Visualize research networks and citation patterns, synthesize evidence across multiple papers, and generate systematic summaries and comparisons.
3. **Organization and Planning (NotebookLM + Zotero):** Organize research materials comprehensively, plan research methodology and approach, and create structured research documentation.
4. **Analysis and Results (Julius AI + SciSpace):** Conduct data analysis and generate visualizations, interpret results in the context of existing literature, and develop comprehensive results presentations.
5. **Writing and Editing (Jenni + Grammarly):** Draft thesis chapters with AI assistance, enhance writing quality and academic tone, and ensure proper citation and formatting.
6. **Quality Assurance and Publication (Turnitin + PaperPal):** Verify originality and academic integrity, prepare manuscripts for submission, and optimize for publication requirements.

Cross-Platform Workflows: Develop systematic approaches that combine multiple AI tools effectively, ensuring that tools complement rather than compete with each other in research workflows. Learn to move data and insights seamlessly between different AI platforms, creating comprehensive research environments that leverage the strengths of multiple tools.

Scalability Planning: Develop research workflows that can adapt to larger projects, collaborative research, and evolving technological capabilities.

Start your pipeline with Semantic Scholar and Zotero, automating tasks to enhance efficiency and scalability.

3.5 Collaborative Research Integration

Collaborative research benefits from AI tools that streamline teamwork and advisor feedback for graduate students.

Thesis Guide or Advisor Integration

- Share research progress through platform-specific sharing features.
- Create systematic approaches for advisor review and feedback.
- Use collaborative features for real-time research guidance.
- Develop procedures for incorporating advisor feedback systematically.
- Create documentation systems that support advisor oversight.
- Establish regular review cycles using collaborative platform features.

Preparing for Your Future Career Developments:

- **Skill Development:** Focus on developing skills in AI tool evaluation and adoption. Build capabilities in workflow design and optimization. Develop expertise in quality assurance for AI-assisted research. Cultivate leadership skills in ethical AI use and community standards.
- **Community Engagement:** Participate in research communities focused on AI tool development. Contribute to open source projects that support research automation. Share experiences and best practices with emerging tool users. Engage with tool developers to influence future development directions.
- **Ethical Leadership:** Develop frameworks for evaluating new tools against ethical standards. Create guidelines that can adapt to emerging technological capabilities. Build expertise in balancing efficiency gains with academic integrity. Cultivate skills in teaching others about responsible AI use.
- **Research Positioning:** Position research at the intersection of human expertise and AI capabilities. Develop research approaches that leverage emerging AI capabilities. Build expertise that will remain valuable as AI capabilities advance. Create research programs that can adapt to technological change.

The future of AI-enhanced research will require researchers who can thoughtfully integrate emerging technologies while maintaining the fundamental values of scholarly inquiry. The foundation provided in this guide will support adaptation to new tools and capabilities as they emerge.

Start with Zotero's group libraries at zotero.org to collaborate with advisors and peers, streamlining teamwork for impactful research.

3.6 Next-Generation AI Research Capabilities

Next-generation AI tools will provide even more sophisticated understanding of research content, enabling more nuanced analysis and synthesis capabilities. Emerging tools will integrate text, visual, and audio content seamlessly, supporting more comprehensive research approaches. Advanced platforms will enable real-time collaborative research across global teams with sophisticated coordination and communication capabilities. Future tools will provide more comprehensive automation of research processes while maintaining human control over critical decisions.

Advanced Natural Language Understanding: Current AI tools represent early stages of natural language processing capabilities. Emerging developments promise even more sophisticated understanding of research content:

- **Contextual Research Understanding:** Future AI tools will better understand research context, including disciplinary conventions, theoretical frameworks, and methodological traditions. This enhanced understanding will enable more nuanced suggestions and analysis.
- **Longitudinal Research Analysis:** Advanced tools will track research development over time, identifying trends, predicting future directions, and suggesting research opportunities based on historical patterns and emerging developments.
- **Cross-Modal Integration:** Next-generation tools will integrate text, image, audio, and video content seamlessly, supporting more comprehensive research approaches that incorporate diverse data types.

Multimodal Research Support:

- **Visual Research Integration:** Emerging tools will analyze research images, diagrams, and visualizations as sophisticated as text analysis, enabling comprehensive understanding of research content across different presentation formats.
- **Audio and Video Analysis:** Advanced platforms will process interview recordings, lecture content, and video data with the same sophistication currently available for text analysis.
- **Interactive Research Environments:** Future tools will create immersive research environments where researchers can explore data and literature through virtual and augmented reality interfaces.

Collaborative Intelligence Platforms:

- **Global Research Networks:** Advanced platforms will connect researchers worldwide through AI-mediated collaboration that transcends language, cultural, and institutional barriers.
- **Intelligent Project Management:** AI systems will provide sophisticated project management that adapts to research progress, identifies potential problems early, and suggests optimization strategies.
- **Automated Research Coordination:** Future tools will coordinate complex research projects automatically, managing timelines, resources, and collaboration while maintaining human oversight and control.

Preparing for Future Developments:

- **Skill Development Strategies:** Focus on developing meta-skills in tool evaluation and adoption. Build expertise in workflow design and optimization. Cultivate leadership capabilities in ethical AI use. Develop teaching skills to help others adopt AI tools effectively.

- **Community Engagement:** Participate in research communities focused on AI tool development. Contribute to open source projects supporting research automation. Share experiences and best practices with emerging technology users. Engage with tool developers to influence future development directions.
- **Professional Positioning:** Position research at the intersection of human expertise and AI capabilities. Develop unique capabilities that combine traditional research skills with AI integration. Build a reputation as an ethical leader in AI-enhanced research. Create research programs that demonstrate the value of human-AI collaboration.

Start exploring next-gen tools to prepare for transformative research capabilities.

In Conclusion, the integration of AI tools marks a transformative era in graduate research, offering unprecedented opportunities to streamline workflows and enhance the quality and impact of scholarly work. This chapter has provided a comprehensive guide to selecting and implementing AI-powered solutions across every stage of the research process—from initial discovery and literature review to methodology development, data analysis, and final manuscript preparation. By strategically adopting tools like Semantic Scholar for discovery, Zotero for citation management, Julius AI for data analysis, and Grammarly for writing, graduate students can significantly boost efficiency, minimize errors, and ensure academic rigor.

Effective implementation hinges on a structured approach, as outlined in the 12-week checklist, which emphasizes systematic setup, integration, and validation. While AI tools offer immense advantages, proactive troubleshooting is crucial to address common challenges related to access, integration, and accuracy. Furthermore, advanced integration strategies enable the creation of seamless research pipelines, fostering greater scalability and collaboration among researchers and advisors. The future of AI in research promises even more sophisticated capabilities, including advanced natural language understanding, multimodal support, and intelligent collaborative platforms, underscoring the importance of continuous skill development and ethical considerations.

Ultimately, mastering AI tools is not about replacing human intellect but augmenting it. By thoughtfully integrating artificial intelligence with human expertise, graduate students can navigate the complexities of modern research more effectively, produce high-impact publications, and position themselves as leaders in the evolving academic landscape. The journey into AI-enhanced research is dynamic, requiring adaptability and a commitment to ethical practice. Embracing these tools and strategies will empower a new generation of scholars to push the boundaries of knowledge and address humanity's most pressing challenges.

Chapter 4

Conclusion: The Future of AI-Enhanced Research

The integration of artificial intelligence into academic research signifies more than a technological advancement; it represents a fundamental transformation in how we generate, analyze, and disseminate knowledge. This comprehensive guide has provided frameworks, tools, and strategies to navigate this shift while upholding the highest standards of scholarly integrity and research quality.

The journey of AI-enhanced research is truly just beginning. The tools and techniques presented herein offer a foundational framework for continuous development and adaptation as new technologies emerge and research challenges evolve. The ultimate aim is not to supplant human intelligence with artificial intelligence, but to forge powerful partnerships that enable more comprehensive, efficient, and insightful scholarship.

As we look toward the future, several key principles will be paramount in guiding successful AI integration:

- **Human-Centered Design:** AI tools must always serve human purposes and values, enhancing rather than diminishing human judgment, creativity, and insight. The most successful AI integration maintains human control over research direction while leveraging technological capabilities for efficiency and comprehensiveness.

- **Ethical Leadership:** The research community bears a significant responsibility to develop and uphold ethical standards for AI use. This ensures the preservation of academic integrity while simultaneously fostering innovation. Such an endeavor necessitates ongoing dialogue, policy development, and strong community leadership.
- **Continuous Adaptation:** The rapidly evolving technological landscape demands that researchers cultivate the ability to adapt swiftly to new tools and capabilities. This must be done while consistently maintaining research quality and adhering to ethical standards. Such adaptability will be a critical skill for future research success.
- **Collaborative Excellence:** AI-enhanced research inherently involves collaboration across diverse disciplines, institutions, and cultural boundaries. Success in this environment requires the continuous development of skills in collaboration, communication, and cultural sensitivity.
- **Quality Commitment:** Irrespective of technological sophistication, research quality remains the paramount concern. AI tools must invariably enhance, not compromise, the rigor, accuracy, and reliability that are the hallmarks of excellent scholarship.

Researchers who master these principles will be exceptionally well-positioned to lead the next generation of scholarly inquiry. They will be instrumental in generating knowledge that addresses humanity's most pressing challenges, all while preserving the intellectual traditions that have guided academic excellence for centuries.

The future belongs to researchers capable of thoughtfully integrating human intelligence and artificial intelligence, thereby creating scholarship that is both rigorously traditional and innovatively modern. This guide serves as the foundational stepping stone for that integration, empowering a new generation of scholars to define the future of academic research.

Your journey into AI-enhanced research commences now. The tools, strategies, and principles outlined in this guide will undoubtedly evolve as you apply them to your unique research challenges and opportunities. The objective is not to follow these recommendations mechanically, but to adapt and refine them as you cultivate your own distinct approach to AI-enhanced scholarship.

The future of research does not lie in choosing between human and artificial intelligence, but rather in their thoughtful and strategic integration. By mastering the concepts and tools presented in this guide, you join a vibrant community of scholars who are actively shaping new possibilities for academic excellence in the digital age.

Welcome to the future of research using the Five-Chapter Model. The journey of discovery awaits.

References

Korrapati, Raghu. (2017). *FIVE CHAPTER MODEL RESEARCH THESIS WRITING: 108 Practical Lessons For MS/MBA/M.Tech/M.Phil/LLM, Ph.D Students*. Diamond Pocket Books Pvt Ltd.

Korrapati, Raghu. (2021). *ACADEMIC PUBLISHING: Terminology, Best Practices, Ethics, and Avoiding Publication Misconduct.* Diamond Pocket Books Pvt Ltd.

Korrapati, Raghu. (2022). *ANYONE CAN DO A Ph.D: SUCCESSFUL STRATEGIES TO COMPLETE A PHD PROGRAM.* Diamond Pocket Books Pvt Ltd.

Other Books by Dr. Raghu Korrapati

What is civilization if not a vast and interlinked network of human relationships? With 'The Business of People', Dr Raghu sets out to teach the reader how to make these relationships healthy and mutually beneficial. Dr. Raghu discusses certain characteristics that we all understand but fail to recognise their importance like punctuality, humility, politeness, rationality, prudence, self-supervision, persistence, apologising, assertiveness, taking the initiative, and sense of humour among others.

ISBN-10: 9350832577 **ISBN-13: 978-9350832578**

Validated management Practices will walk you through the 108 required knowledge and skill areas so that you can develop to balance the 3 critical aspects of management-employees, customers and financials well. While some of the chapters in this book are oriented towards managers working in an Information Technology industry, it will be useful for managers in any industry with practical advice and tips on how to become an effective manager. In addition, the appendices contain extract of mandatory skills for all professionals from Dr Raghu's previous books - '108 pearls of Wisdom' and 'Dr Raghu's Top Ten' - his guiding principles.

ISBN-10: 9351654834 **ISBN-13: 978-9351654834**

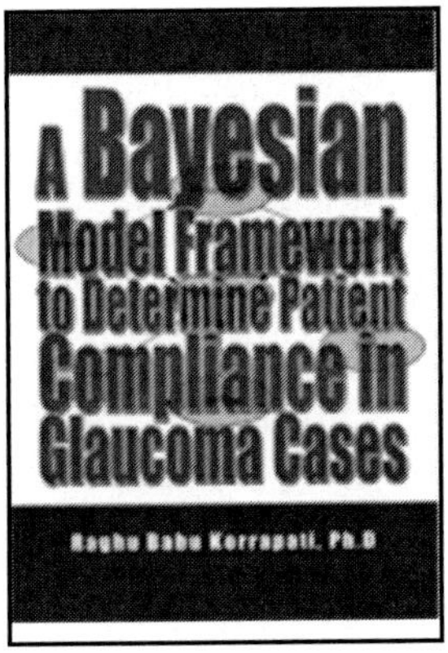

This research applied Bayesian Modeling to medication noncompliance in glaucoma patients. A model-based decision support system using a Bayesian Network was developed to determine whether a patient was complying with the medications prescribed by the physician. The model may be generalized to other business situations where a decision has to be made based on incomplete and uncertain data sets. The purpose of this research was to devise a Bayesian framework to assess the compliance with medication in glaucoma patients.

ISBN-13: 978-0595368396 **ISBN-10: 0595368395**

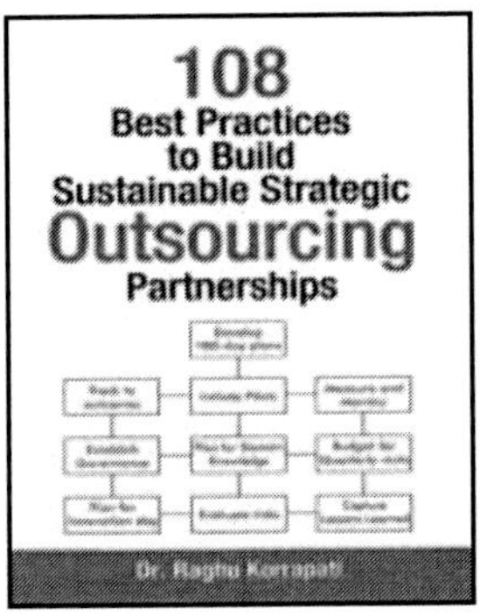

This book is the essence of Dr Korrapati's 30 years of business management experience with highly successful multinational companies, coupled with distilled knowledge of his close interactions with great industry leaders. The book covers - developing a solid outsourcing strategy, deciding what to outsource, negotiating a good deal, keeping the engagement on track, ensuring access to the vendors' best resources, or even terminating a deal in a way that does not harm you. It will benefit everyone, whether you are from a firm that is looking to outsource or a vendor who seeks to establish his company as first choice partner for clients, to gain the advantage you are looking for in the fiercely competitive marketplace.

ASIN: B01JFV7JQM

Leading an organization and its people to success remains a challenge for most managers. With organizations evolving and changing constantly it becomes even more difficult. Management theories and principles often do not provide solutions to the dilemmas that a manager has to deal with in the workplace.

This book by Dr Raghu very adeptly gives some solid answers that managers have sought to be more successful at what they do.

ISBN-10: 8128837575 **ISBN-13: 978-8128837579**

While Dr Raghu Korrapati's 'Passage through India - A tryst with my soul' is an amalgam of Indian experiences of this widely travelled management guru, it is simultaneously also an exposition of his philosophical and spiritual ideas. So, as readers learn numerous lessons in sound management practice presented through Dr Raghu the leader's anecdotes and observations, he/she will be delighted to connect with Dr Raghu the man. Those familiar with Dr Raghu's previous works will be enthralled with another masterpiece on the art and science of management, this time in the context of the master's sojourn as the leader of an India IT organization. 'Passage through India' will, however, will also appeal to those who wish to understand the composer behind the composition, i.e, the mind of a man who successfully runs a large corporate organization.

ISBN-10: 9350836823 **ISBN-13: 978-9350836828**

There is often a considerable gap between the aspirations that many college graduates harbor and the way they go about achieving their goals. While education and technical expertise are often ignore and that defines the difference between an average and a successful career. Dr. Raghu Korrapati has taken it upon himself to identify this 'soft' element and painstakingly elaborated upon its numerous facets. The result is this path-breaking book, which highlights the soft skills that every young graduate and professional needs to possess to reach the pinnacle of professional success. The 108 pearls of wisdom presented here have been drawn from sources as eclectic and diverse as Greek, Indian, Buddhist philosophies, modern day management theory, and psychology. This book has been translated into many languages.

ISBN-10: 8128834223 **ISBN-13: 978-8128834226**

Listed in Best Seller Category

Dr Raghu Korrapati's newest book is a seminal work that is bound to be soon accepted as a significant and powerful contribution to the literature on higher education. This is his landmark effort to encapsulate in one place all that a research scholar might need during his/her research, be it on any subject or discipline. The result is a complex and nuanced picture of the nature, processes, and contexts of research scholarship in varied departmental, disciplinary and institutional cultures.

Undoubtedly, this pivotal and pioneering book will prove to be valuable to both faculty and graduate students who study higher education. Further, institutional leaders, deans, and chairpersons of tenure, and promotion committees who seek to develop vaster comprehension of scholarship will also greatly benefit from this.

Dr Korrapati has mentored thousands of research students in a wide spectrum of disciplines and fields over the span of several decades. This book by him is the latest in a long line of works that have inspired and informed innumerable students and professionals across countries.

ISBN-10: 9352617614 **ISBN-13: 9789352617616**

A Master Service Agreement (MSA) is a contractual document that specifies performance objectives and outlines the responsibilities of both parties in the agreement. It also lists the current and prospective services to which the agreement applies. MSAs typically state performance objectives as service level agreements – written, measurable processes or service performance targets that the service provider and customer agree on. A statement of work (SOW) is a formal document that captures and defines the work activities, deliverables, and timeline a vendor must execute in performance of specified work for a client. The present study attempted to ascertain the factors in developing MSAs and SOWs and various best practices for alternate dispute resolutions available for offshore software managers. The study adds to the body of knowledge in the areas of Software Intellectual Property Rights, Alignment of MSAs and SOWs, ADR Mechanism for Contractual Breaches, Best Practices in Information Technology, Offshore Management, and Organizational Behavior.

ISBN-10: 1532020686 **ISBN-13: 978-1532020681**

The admission of foreign students to universities and colleges in the United States has two major components: the evaluation of foreign educational credentials, and the administrative process that converts an applicant for admission into an enrolled student. The first component has historically been a source of much ambiguity and trouble to Indian students and professionals vying for places in USA Universities.

Dr Raghu Korrapati, in another glorious attempt at championing the cause of students and young professionals all over India, has come up with this seminal work to eliminate this ambiguity. In this ground-breaking new book, he displays rare acumen, insight, and scholarly prowess to minutely analyse the education systems in the USA and India, before going on to provide painstakingly researched information on each Indian higher education degree and its equivalency with respect to USA degrees. For this reason alone, this book is worth its weight in gold for any Indian student planning to study in the USA or an Indian professional aiming to work in the USA.

Apart from the students, there are numerous other institutions and individuals who will benefit from the wonderful content present in the book – USA admission officers and universities, USA employers hiring Indians on H1B visas, licensors, USA state/federal agencies, and immigration attorneys. The amount of detail on the USA education system that has been offered by the matchless Dr Korrapati will also help Indian educational administrators.

ISBN-10: 9352619870 **ISBN-13: 978-93-5261-987-0**

H-1B visas play a very important role in hiring foreign born skilled workers for Specialty Occupations in the United States. This visa system has largely benefited the U.S economy, benefitting the I.T industry the most, with the flow of skilled foreign-born employees. Due to the growing concerns over misuse and a perceived threat to domestic jobs, stricter scrutiny on H-1B petitions has increased in the past few years.

This book aims at demystifying the myths surrounding "Specialty Occupations" not only to the employers, but also to petitioners, academics, attorneys, students and other interested parties. It also aims at filling the gap in the research and understanding on Specialty Occupations. There is no comprehensive text or authority on this important issue and all the information available is only through the policy memoranda of USCIS, judgments in appealed petitioners and blogs of attorneys.

This book tries to provide a better understanding of the issue and also identifies some common errors in H-1B petitions and aims to be a one-stop reference to employers, attorneys and expert opinion evaluators on the issue.

ISBN-10: 9352787708 **ISBN-13: 978-93-5278-770-8**

This book is updated version of previous years book. Based on receiving huge compliments from prior version, this book includes updates for current year. Several new guidelines in the area of Minimum Requirements for proffered position, Interview requirements for Specialty occupations questionnaire, sample job description templates, Guidelines on generic "Engineering" or "Business Administration" degrees, and new requirements for evaluators.

This book aims at demystifying the myths surrounding "Specialty Occupations" not only to the employers, but also to petitioners, academics, attorneys, students and other interested parties. It also aims at filling the gap in the research and understanding on Specialty Occupations. There is no comprehensive text or authority on this important issue and all the information available is only through the policy memoranda of USCIS, judgments in appealed petitioners and blogs of attorneys.

This book tries to provide a better understanding of the issue and also identifies some common errors in H-1B petitions and aims to be a one-stop reference to employers, attorneys and expert opinion evaluators on the issue.

ISBN-10: 9352969227 **ISBN-13: 978-93-5296-922-7**

There is tremendous ambiguity surrounding this field. It is compounded by the fact that grading systems differ widely in theory and practice from one country to another, and the fair interpretation of foreign grades into national ones is a major concern, both for students returning after a study period abroad and for university staff required to assess the credentials of foreign applicants. The academic world, especially students, struggle to determine what their education amounts to in another country.

The credential evaluation component also exists outside of the academic community: at state licensing boards and other types of governmental agencies, at professional associations, and at private foreign educational credential evaluation services which assist institutions and agencies that do not have in-house expertise. This book is also aimed to facilitate the smoother functioning of these institutions.

ISBN-10: 9352969219 **ISBN-13: 978-93-5296-921-0**

It is often said that salespeople would rather sell than spend a day learning how to do it. They think time is money and every hour spent in training is money lost and time wasted. But what they fail to understand is that learning how to do sales effectively is actually a catalyst for great sales results for the organization and excellent sales performance for the individual. It is worth noting that while sales is one of the easiest careers to get into, it is not as easy to sustain and spend a life in. So to put it in simpler words, ***"Everyone can be a sales person, but not everyone can be a successful sales person".*** To be a successful salesperson it is important to have a deep understanding of the industry you cater to. While the general skill set remains the same, it is the deeper and niche understanding that has the power to differentiate the best from the rest.

In the market, there are numerous books and articles on various sales techniques available. In this book, I am discussing the 'Nine habits of highly effective software sales professionals'. The title gives you a broad idea of what this book is all about, but more than nine habits, it is packed with 30 years of my personal and professional experience in the software industry and managing clients. I provided more emphasis on how successful sales professionals, sales leaders and their companies organize themselves with short-term and long-term planning and adopt disciplined execution on those plans.

ISBN-10: 9352969200 **ISBN-13: 978-93-5296-920-3**

"Academic Publishing" by Dr Raghu Korrapati is a comprehensive guide to provide deep insights into academic publishing and how to avoid costly pitfalls. Being a scholar practitioner and publisher himself with over three decades years of academic and executive leadership work experience, Dr Korrapati has distilled key facets of academic publishing into nine core chapters ranging from the step-by-step process of academic publication to measuring the impact of published work while focusing on publication ethics and avoiding misconduct. Each chapter provides guiding principles and builds the foundation toward guiding you to become a successful scholar-publisher. Use this book as a guide to help you navigate the path toward becoming a great scholar publisher.

ISBN-10: 9355990405 ISBN-13: 978-93-5599-040-2

For many international students, pursuing higher education in the United States is a dream come true. However, navigating the complex regulations of maintaining F1 student visa status, and transitioning to H-1B status can be complex and daunting for many students. As an F1 visa holder, you are required to maintain your student status to remain in the United States legally. Failure to comply with these regulations can result in serious consequences, including the revocation of your visa and even deportation. There have been spikes in the number of Request for Evidences (RFEs) issued during the H-1B applications adjudication process. This is due to lack of evidence submitted by the petitioners to prove their compliance in maintaining the F1 (and OPT/CPT) statuses. Often, this also results in H-1B petition denial, forcing the students to wait multiple years for their H-1B visa.

This book is designed to guide F1 visa students to understand the requirements for maintaining their student status and provide practical guidance on how to stay compliant with these regulations whether you are enrolled in a University, or undergoing OPT (or CPT), or planning to transition to H-1B visa. Whether you are a first-time international student or have been studying in the United States for some time, this book offers valuable insights into the nuances of F1 visa regulations.

The author, Dr Raghu Korrapati, draws upon his extensive experience working with international students and navigating the US visa system. With clear, concise language and actionable advice, this book is an essential resource for any international student seeking to maximize their educational experience in the United States while maintaining legal status, complying with regulations, and achieving their career goals.

ISBN-13: 978-93-5964-832-3

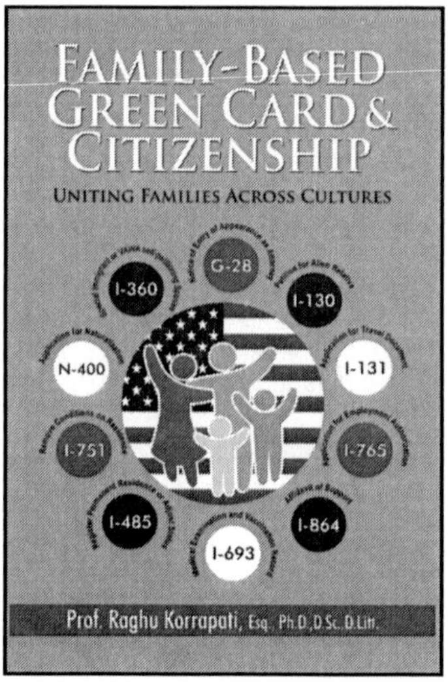

Family-based Green Card and Citizenship: Uniting Families Across Cultures is more than just a collection of legal procedures and paperwork-it's a testament to the power of family, love, and the unwavering human spirit. It's a tribute to the countless individuals who have dared to dream, to hope, and to believe in the promise of a brighter future. This book is packed with practical advices, expert insights, and actionable strategies to navigate the complex and often daunting process of family-based immigration. From understanding the legal requirements to overcoming common challenges, this book is your roadmap to successfully reuniting with your loved ones and building a new life in America.

Though this book offers valuable information and guidance, it is not a substitute for legal advice. Immigration laws and procedures are subject to change, and each case may have specific circumstances that need professional legal help. Therefore, it's advisable to consult a qualified immigration attorney or accredited representative for personalized assistance with your immigration journey.

ISBN-13: 978-93-5964-832-3

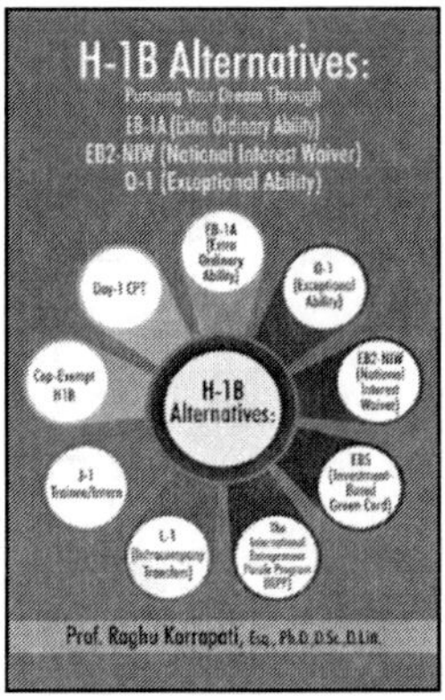

Embark on a transformative journey with "H-1B Alternatives: Pursuing your dream through EB-1A, O-1A, O-1B, and EB-2 NIW." In this meticulously crafted guide, Prof. Raghu Korrapati unveils alternative visa pathways beyond the conventional H-1B route, empowering professionals with the insights and strategies needed to shape their American dreams into reality. Amidst the complexities and uncertainties of the H-1B visa process, Prof. Korrapati presents strategic alternatives, providing insights crucial for informed decision-making. Designed for visionary entrepreneurs, pioneering academics, artists, and seasoned professionals alike, it provides a tailored roadmap to navigate the complexities of U.S. immigration with confidence.

Explore the depths of EB-1A, O-1A, O-1B, and EB-2 NIW visas, where each chapter provides detailed and actionable insights into building your compelling profile toward these alternative visa paths. With meticulous attention to detail, Prof Korrapati analyzes the nuances of each alternative visa category, illuminating the path towards realizing your professional aspirations in the U.S. Armed with curated insights, real-life case studies, and expert strategies, this guide becomes your trusted companion on the journey to success. From crafting a compelling profile to mastering the intricacies of visa interviews, every page is infused with the knowledge and wisdom needed to overcome obstacles and seize opportunities. Let this book be your roadmap to realizing your dreams and making a meaningful contribution to your chosen field in the United States.

ISBN-10: 9363181901 **ISBN-13: 978-93-6318-190-8**

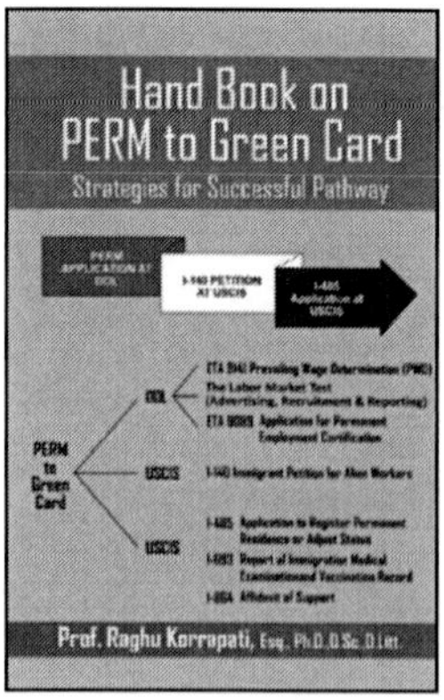

Simplify Your Journey to a USA Green Card with the "Handbook on PERM to Green Card"

Navigate the complex PERM process with confidence and achieve your American dream using **"Handbook on PERM to Green Card – Strategies for a Successful Pathway."** This comprehensive guide breaks down the three critical stages of the PERM/Green Card process:

1. **Meeting USA Department of Labor (DOL) Requirements**
2. **Filing the I-140 Immigrant Petition with USCIS**
3. **Completing the I-485 Adjustment of Status (AOS) with USCIS**

Perfect for employers, legal professionals, and business immigrants, this guide provides clear strategies and actionable steps to simplify each stage of the process.

Learn to master the DOL's three key steps:

- **ETA-9141 Prevailing Wage Determination (PWD)**
- **The Labor Market Test (Advertising, Recruitment & Reporting)**
- **ETA-9089 Application for Permanent Employment Certification**

Gain in-depth knowledge of DOL's Request for Inquiry (RFI), PERM Audit Requests, Letter of Business Necessity, Ability to Pay Justification along with filing the I-140 petition with USCIS, proving qualifications, and demonstrating financial readiness. Finally, tackle the I-485 adjustment of status process with USCIS, securing travel permits and employment authorizations (EAD) without delays.

Packed with expert advice, practical tips, and real-world examples, the **"Handbook on PERM to Green Card"** is your ultimate resource for ensuring compliance, avoiding obstacles, and maximizing your success. Transform your immigration journey into a seamless experience and take the first step toward making your dream a reality.

ASIN: B0DZP1WWLC **ISBN-10: 93-5318-190-8**

Snapshot of Soft Skills!

- Identify your stakeholders and maintain positive relationships with them.
- First impressions are very important.
- Being on time is imperative. This means sticking to the schedule, each time. If you are late, let it be known well in advance.
- Take notes in meetings. You will be surprised what you forget.
- Know your boundaries. Talk with your supervisor about what decisions you should or should not make. Analyze/ review expectations frequently.
- Observe and learn others, yet create your own style. Be careful to not imbibe those traits that are likely to be detrimental.
- Have fun. Make friends. Enjoy what you do.
- Learn from your seniors on how they keep a track of the numerous tasks that they have to accomplish. Having a daily "To do" list helps.
- Before leaving messages on voice mail, write down your message and speak it slowly. For e-mails, learn when to do a "reply all" vs. "reply".
- Make a visible impact in first 100 days of your new role or job.
- Understand that it is OK to do mistakes. Ensure that you don't repeat these mistakes.

- Anything that can be measured statistically can be improved. Find a way to implement measurability.
- Criticize in private and praise in public.
- Follow-up and follow-up some more. It will highlight your dedication like nothing else.
- A hand-written thank you note is far better than an e-mail.
- Differentiate yourself from your competition to provide value to your customers. And remember that both competitors and customers can be internal.
- Plan on Monday morning; then assess and take stock on Friday. Track your weekly status without fail.
- Recommend solutions to problems and challenges and identify opportunities.
- Focus on three sides of the triangle – Employees, Customers, and Understanding your company's Business.
- Awareness on priorities will change on daily/monthly basis. Plan proactively.

Driving Forces of Change

- Make a visible impact in first 100 days.
- On time: Work schedule, meetings, & everything.
- Take notes - keep up with documentation.
- Learn the boundaries of the gig.
- Bring your own style.
- Follow-up / Follow-up / Follow-up.
- Have fun - laugh at the ridiculous.
- The feelers are always up for the train coming - before it hits.
- Drive to solution - everything is done in context of solution.

Dr. Raghu's Top Ten Principles for Success

1. **Embrace Life's Constant Evolution**
   Accept that change is life's only constant. Develop resilience and adaptability rather than resisting inevitable transitions—those who thrive are those who learn to navigate change with grace.

2. **Cultivate Global Connections**
   Build meaningful friendships across cultures and backgrounds. Extract valuable insights from diverse worldviews and traditions—cultural competency is essential for effective leadership in our interconnected world.

3. **Build Strategic Professional Relationships**
   Proactively introduce yourself to managers and key stakeholders. Invest time in understanding their perspectives, priorities, and working styles to create mutually beneficial professional connections.

4. **Expand Your Intellectual Horizons**
   Read voraciously beyond required materials. Explore newspapers, industry journals, magazines, and books that broaden your knowledge base and keep you informed about trends affecting your field and interests.

5. **Travel as Education**
   Use travel as a powerful learning tool to understand both your own culture and others'. Exposure to different environments, people, and perspectives develops empathy and global awareness.

6. **Maximize Every Learning Opportunity**
   Treat time as your most valuable resource. Continuously seek ways to enhance your education and skills—never let a chance for growth pass by unused.

7. **Design Your Personal Blueprint**
   Establish clear annual goals for self-improvement. Create both a personal mission statement that defines your purpose and a compelling vision that guides your long-term direction.

8. **Invest in Relationship Capital**
   Network strategically and authentically. Nurture positive relationships with family, colleagues, and supervisors—your network becomes your professional and personal support system.

9. **Practice Social Responsibility**
   Engage in volunteer activities that give back to your community. Stay connected with your alma mater and remember your roots—social responsibility strengthens both character and community ties.

10. **Create a Meaningful Legacy**
    Leave positive, lasting impacts across all life dimensions—your career, education, and family relationships. Strive to be remembered for contributions that matter and values that inspire others.

Core Message:

Success comes from intentionally developing yourself across multiple dimensions while maintaining strong relationships and contributing meaningfully to the world around you. These principles create a foundation for both personal fulfillment and professional achievement.

Notes

Notes

Notes

Notes

Notes

Notes

Notes